MADWOMEN

MAD

The *Locas mujeres* POEMS
OF GABRIELA MISTRAL

THE UNIVERSITY OF CHICAGO PRESS

WOMEN

A Bilingual Edition

Edited and Translated by **RANDALL COUCH**

CHICAGO AND LONDON

GABRIELA MISTRAL was the pseudonym of Lucila Godoy (1889–1957), born in Vicuña, Chile. A poet, teacher, diplomat, and feminist, she promoted educational reform in Chile and Mexico and served as Chilean consul in Naples, Madrid, Petrópolis, Nice, Lisbon, Santa Barbara, Veracruz, Rapallo, and New York, where she represented Chile at the United Nations. She received the Nobel Prize in Literature in 1945.

RANDALL COUCH is adjunct professor of English at Arcadia University and an administrator at the University of Pennsylvania.

The University of Chicago Press, Chicago 60637
The University of Chicago Press, Ltd., London
© 2008 by The University of Chicago
All rights reserved. Published 2008
Printed in the United States of America

17 16 15 14 13 12 11 10 09 08   1 2 3 4 5

ISBN-13: 978-0-226-53190-8 (cloth)
ISBN-10: 0-226-53190-2 (cloth)

Spanish poems copyright the Estate of Gabriela Mistral.

Library of Congress Cataloging-in-Publication Data

Mistral, Gabriela, 1889-1957.
    Madwomen : the Locas mujeres poems of Gabriela Mistral /
edited and translated by Randall Couch.—A bilingual ed.
        p. cm.
    Includes bibliographical references and index.
    ISBN-13: 978-0-226-53190-8 (cloth : alk. paper)
    ISBN-10: 0-226-53190-2 (cloth : alk. paper)
        1. Mistral, Gabriela, 1889-1957—Translations into
English.   I. Couch, Randall.   II. Title.
    PQ8097.G6A2 2007
    861'.62—dc22
                                        2007025628

♾ The paper used in this publication meets the minimum
requirements of the American National Standard for Information
Sciences—Permanence of Paper for Printed Library Materials,
ANSI Z39.48-1992.

CONTENTS

From *Lagar II*

UNCOLLECTED

ACKNOWLEDGMENTS

This book would not exist but for a chance remark. To Anne Winters, whose quip piqued my interest in translating Mistral's poetry, I owe first thanks.

Taking up the challenge brought me into the company of a remarkable group of scholars whose collegiality has been both a gift and a model. Elizabeth Horan's extraordinary generosity with her time, expertise, and unpublished research strengthened every stage of the work. Marjorie Agosín's encouragement, and her timely invitation to set down my thoughts on the process of translation, inspired me from the start. Her reading of early drafts inflected my approach to Mistral's use of tone, as did that of Patricia Rubio. Persephone Braham applied her lively wit to help me map the cruxes in what became our lunch poems. I'm grateful to them all.

Several poets and translators have read portions of the manuscript at different stages. Reginald Gibbons, Brooks Haxton, and Daniel Tobin each offered detailed and valuable suggestions, as well as the still more valuable example of their own work. I'm honored to have learned from them. Lawrence Venuti, through his theoretical writing and his own translations, has greatly broadened my range as a translator. I'm happily indebted to him for our ongoing conversation.

Friends, artists, and writers with roots in the Southern Cone have also been enormously helpful. Patricia Gherovici shared her analytical acuity and cultural knowledge both early and late in the project. Parts of the manuscript benefited from comments by Nury Vicens and David Preiss. I'm also grateful for responses to specific poems by members of the Yale Poetry Group and, in Philadelphia, the Smedley Street Writers Group.

To Doris Atkinson, niece of Doris Dana and executor of the Mistral estate, I am indebted for her gracious permission to publish and translate the Spanish texts. My thanks to the staff of the Library of

Congress Manuscript Division, especially Alice Birney and Jeffrey Flannery; to Carol Falcione at the Barnard College Library; to the wonderful people at the University of Pennsylvania Library, notably Joseph Holub and Andrea Baruzzi; and to the academic consortia and interlibrary-loan professionals who have enabled me to consult scarce and sometimes fragile materials here at Penn.

I'm grateful to my editor at the University of Chicago Press, Randy Petilos, for his support of this project, to manuscript editor Ruth Goring, and to the Press's outside readers for their helpful comments.

I'd also like to acknowledge the unique literary community formed by the Warren Wilson College MFA program for writers, where Anne Winters happened to overhear a conversation.

To Clare Kinney, for shared pleasures of the imagination and of the understanding, and for her many contributions to this volume, my deepest gratitude.

R. C.
Philadelphia, 2007

INTRODUCTION

My friend, I know what I do intuitively; I don't have the knack of other writers, who can expound on their traits or their tricks like someone lecturing from a chair in mineralogy. Each poem is an adventure with new paths, including unknown animals and weapons. And one has to invent at full speed a bow capable of felling the incandescent meteor coming down on us or the vertiginous bird that circles us. I start from an emotion that little by little is put into words, helped by a rhythm that could be that of my own heart. You will smile, knowing my tachycardia. . . . But aren't many of my poems, especially those in Lagar, *riding a runaway heart?[1]*

Written at the height of her powers, the *Locas mujeres* poems associated with Gabriela Mistral's final collection *Lagar* (Winepress) rank among the poet's most challenging and compelling work. As her letter to the writer Fedor Ganz suggests, they are poems of the self *in extremis,* marked by the wound of blazing catastrophe and its aftermath of mourning. Mistral bends the bow of poetry, a frail weapon against the unhinging of consciousness, into strange new forms.

In contrast to her first book, *Desolación,* these poems do not perform loss and longing in a florid or sentimental style. The poet has also largely laid aside the pastoral mission that played such a large part

---

1 "Amigo mio, yo sé intuitivamente lo que hago; no tengo esa ciencia de otros escritores, que pueden exponer sus rasgos o sus trucos como quien dicta una cátedra de mineralogía. Cada poema es una aventura con rutas nuevas, incluso con armas y animales desconocidos. Y hay que inventar a toda prisa el arco capaz de tumbar al bólido incandescente que se nos viene encima o al ave vertiginosa que nos anilla. Parto de una emoción que poco a poco se pone en palabras, ayudada por un ritmo que pudiera ser el de mi propio corazón. Usted sonreirá, conociéndome mis taquicardias. . . . Pero, ¿acaso no están muchos de mis poemas, más que todos los de *Lagar,* a caballo de un corazón desbocado?" Gabriela Mistral to Fedor Ganz, 4 January 1955, in *Cartas,* vol. 3 of *Gabriela Mistral: Antología mayor* (Santiago: Cochrane, 1992), 574–75.

in the growth of her influence and reputation.² The tone of moral security, of tender didacticism, of speaking from safety on behalf of the childlike and vulnerable, is gone.

Instead, the poet's inner turmoil is palpable. Some of the pieces display a weird humor. Balladlike and folkloric elements are ironized. Many enact a tragic sense of life—explicitly so in the four poems voiced by Greek dramatic heroines. These madwomen are strong, intensely human beings confronting situations to which no sane response exists. To some extent they project Mistral's own experience, but they continue to resonate in an age of suicide bombers and secret prisons.

Throughout her career Mistral grouped her poems according to descriptive rubrics, often adding new pieces under the same series title in subsequent volumes. The *Locas mujeres* series was inaugurated in *Lagar,* but at the poet's death several additional poems—some published in periodicals, some still in typescript or manuscript—remained uncollected. *Madwomen* brings together twenty-six works in a bilingual edition that presents the series whole. While some of the uncollected material retains marks from the chisel and the file, it also includes some of the poet's finest writing.

More than that of most artists, Gabriela Mistral's poetry has suffered from simple-minded biographical criticism. Yet she was one of the twentieth century's most fascinating international figures, and a sense of her intellectual development and eventful life helps to illuminate the work. In the following pages I will present a brief biographical sketch, followed by observations on Mistral's poetic technique and some notes on the translations. A discussion of my source texts follows the poems.

LIVES OF THE POET

Recent biographical scholarship has been crucial in recognizing the rhetorical sophistication of Mistral's poetic compositions. Writers such as Patricia Rubio, Elizabeth Horan, and Licia Fiol-Matta have used Mistral's letters and prose writings to demonstrate the poet's

---

2 Licia Fiol-Matta applies Michel Foucault's concept of the "pastoral power" of the state to Mistral's *canciones de cuna* and other writings that participate in nation building and gender-role construction in *A Queer Mother for the Nation* (Minneapolis: University of Minnesota Press, 2002), 120.

acute consciousness of the small number of authoritative positions from which she—as a woman in a male-controlled literary and political culture and as a product of the rural middle class—might speak. They show Mistral cultivating not just one but several distinct audiences, adjusting her self-presentation, her literary persona, and the rhetoric of her poems to reach and persuade each one. This work provides an important corrective to the popular picture of "Saint Gabriela" as a kind of naive, divinely inspired "natural." It's no derogation of her achievement, no contradiction of her ethics, to recall that her very literary self—the name Gabriela Mistral—was both an indirection and a fabrication.

Genesis, Exodus

Gabriela Mistral was born Lucila Godoy in the Elqui valley of Chile's Norte Chico region in 1889. Located in the foothills between the coastal town of La Serena and the Andean cordillera, the Valley of Elqui then as now was famous for its cloudless skies and natural beauty. The nostalgic, Edenic image of the valley figured in the poet's work as it did in the country's cultural mythology.[3] But daily life in paradise was another thing. Most of the arable land and its limited water supply were controlled by a few families. The majority of the population consisted of landless laborers, with a small rural middle class struggling to emerge amid rapid changes in the nation's economy and demography.

Northern Chile at the end of the nineteenth century was the world's principal supplier of nitrate, essential for compounding fertilizers and explosives. The expanding nitrate market created a demand for miners in the north, while recycled nitrate profits drove rapid industrialization and growth in the urban centers. Along with government-sponsored colonization of the agricultural south, these forces caused widespread social dislocations as men left their families looking for work. The poet's household during her childhood, like many at the time, consisted of women and children who moved often

---

3 "El saber de los viejos contiene mucha agriura. Es como el limón ácido. . . . Fui feliz en el valle de Elqui y después ya no lo fui mas." (The wisdom of old people contains much bitterness. It's sour as a lemon. . . . I was happy in the Valley of Elqui and later on I wasn't anymore.) Gabriela Mistral to Matilde Ladrón de Guevara, 1951, in Cartas, 526.

to pursue transient employment, while the men wandered farther away.[4] The impact of this male flight can be seen in the poems "La abandonada" and "La granjera" in this volume.

Mistral's own father, an itinerant schoolteacher and musician who had a seminarian's education, abandoned his family when she was three. Romanticized by Mistral's early biographers as a picaresque troubadour, Jerónimo Godoy was believed by his daughter to have been an alcoholic.[5] From him she later claimed to have received traits she associated with both the Basque and indigenous strains of her *mestiza* heritage. His mother, Mistral's paternal grandmother Isabel Villanueva, lived in the old coastal town of La Serena, having left her own landowning husband because of his infidelity. In old age she stayed in a room given her by nuns, since her daughters had both entered convents themselves, leaving no one to care for her. Late in life, Mistral recalled visiting her on Saturdays and finding her in a "curious mental state. She wasn't crazy; I never saw her violent but she was constantly delirious."[6] Isabel was devoted to the Bible and its poetry and taught her young granddaughter to "repeat the psalms of '*my Father David.*' . . . From her came my love of the Bible; I would not have had it without her."[7]

As a child the poet was quiet and aloof. She was taught informally by her stepsister Emelina, an elementary-school teacher who had become the family's breadwinner. An attempt to enroll the child in a

---

4 The following biographical summary draws heavily on the work of Elizabeth Horan. Except where otherwise noted, or where referring to well-known facts, the narrative follows that of her forthcoming biography of the poet and her 1994 study *Gabriela Mistral: An Artist and Her People.* I am indebted to her for sharing the results of her archival research and her knowledge of Mistral's correspondence. Except where quoting from English-language sources or as otherwise noted, translations from the Spanish are mine.

5 "Ya se había dado al licor y mi madre y mi hermana solo sosegaban cuando el partía." (He had already been given to drink, and my mother and sister were only relieved when he left.) Gabriela Mistral to Radomiro Tomic, Olaya Errázuriz Tomic, and family, February(?) 1954, in *Vuestra Gabriela: Cartas inéditas de Gabriela Mistral,* edited by Luis Vargas Saavedra (Santiago: Zig-Zag), 228.

6 "Vivía en La Serena en una habitación cedida por unas monjas y en un curioso estado mental. No estaba loca; nunca le vi una violencia, pero deliraba constantamente." Ibid., 225.

7 "Yo iba a verla cada sábado. Me pedía cada vez que yo quisiese a mi padre 'a pesar de todo' y me hacía repetir los Salmos de '*mi padre David.*' . . . Fue de ella de donde me vino el amor de la Biblia; no la habría yo tenido sin ella." Ibid.

nearby school ended traumatically when she was accused, apparently unjustly, of stealing supplies and was dismissed. An appeal was denied on the basis that the girl had no intellectual gifts and was suited only for domestic tasks. Emelina provided the remainder of the poet's schooling in her scarce free time. The family relocated several times in the next few years as Emelina married, was widowed, and returned to teaching. The adolescent Mistral, stubbornly resisting the label she'd been given, became a "dreamer," useless for housework, always scribbling in notebooks.

But for the people of Elqui it was "starve or work, everyone, men, women, and children."[8] In 1904, Mistral's mother appealed to a local school inspector and managed to place the fifteen-year-old girl as an aide in the school of Compañía Baja, a seaside town near La Serena.

In provincial towns where books were scarce and paper was rationed in schools, newspapers bore the burden of print culture. Their daily need for copy provided opportunities for local writers. Within a year of arriving in Compañía Baja, Mistral had published in several area papers: extravagantly melancholic meditations in prose and verse, "diary" pages, and "intimate letters," as well as nonfiction commentaries and occasional pieces. These publications elicited printed responses—some flattering, some engaging the author in controversy. Despite her lurid and romanticized style, the teenager forcefully argued against the view that women should be merely decorative and moral and asserted her commitment to "the intellectual light, the light of glory."[9] Local papers began to commission work from her, and gradually she gained entry to provincial literary and political circles. She acquired a crucial friend and sponsor in Bernardo Ossandón, a newspaper publisher, educational activist, Radical Party politician, and former mayor. Ossandón possessed a good library and allowed the poet to borrow from it freely. In her

8 "Allí no queda sino hambrearse o trabajar todos, hombres, mujeres y niños." Gabriela Mistral, "Breve descripción de Chile (Conferencia dada en Málaga, España)," in *Recados: Contando a Chile* (Santiago: Editorial del Pacífico, 1957); reprinted in Hernán Godoy Urzúa, ed., *El carácter Chileno: Estudio preliminar y selección de ensayos* (Santiago: Editorial Universitaria, 1976), 54.

9 "Hay almas que, saliendo de la mediocridad, no esperan ver iluminarse aquel con los fulgores de dos ojos apasionados, sino con la luz única que existe sobre la Tierra, la luz intelectual, la luz de la gloria." Lucila Godoy in *La Voz de Elqui*, Vicuña, 26 November 1905, reprinted in Pedro Pablo Zegers, ed., *Recopilación de la obra Mistraliana 1902–1922* (Santiago, RIL Editores, 2002), 91.

bare, dirt-floored room she began, in the hours after school, the life of reading that would form her real education.

Ossandón and others arranged for the poet to take an administrative position in the best girls' school in the area, the Liceo de Niñas in La Serena, in 1907, so that she could take classes, but she was asked to resign after a difference with the school's German director. Undaunted, she attempted to enroll in La Serena's Normal School but was asked to leave after a brief stay. Mistral later gave differing accounts of this exclusion, emphasizing variously her progressive political views, religious independence, and rustic nativism as affronting the school's Catholic chaplain and its American director.

Once more luck and fellow writers favored the unemployed girl. On a train she met the governor of Coquimbo, himself a poet, who offered her a job teaching in the tiny village of La Cantera. There she organized a night school while continuing to publish in local newspapers. In 1908 her work was included, under the name Lucila Godoy, in a regional anthology, *Literatura Coquimbana*.

In the same year she also began using the pseudonym Gabriela Mistral. At this time even upper-class women writers in Chile employed pseudonyms as a screening gesture, a transparent concession intended to preserve the names and reputations of fathers and husbands. Inés Bello Echeverria de Larraín, for example, wrote as "Iris." Lucila Godoy chose another divine messenger for the first part of her nom de plume, coupling it with the fierce Mediterranean wind in a binomial construction that satisfied convention but also created a plausible civil form. Indeed, as her fame grew, she came to use her given names rarely and only for specific purposes. At the time she adopted "Gabriela Mistral," its associations with the regionalist and late romantic authors Gabriele d'Annunzio and Frédéric Mistral would have been consistent with her poetic aspirations; later in life she no longer emphasized them.

Early Fame: *Los sonetos de la muerte*

In 1909 Mistral transferred from La Cantera to the railroad town of Cerillos, which allowed her to travel to the province's major cities and brought her into contact with a young railroad employee named Romelio Ureta. Mistral's later accounts cast her in the role of one of two women in Ureta's life—either onlooker or rival to his fiancée.[10] Ureta committed suicide, an act attributed by a contemporary newspaper to his being confronted with having embezzled funds.[11] Popular belief assigned the cause to amorous conflict. Ureta's suicide provided the background to Mistral's macabre, elaborately performed trio of poems *Los sonetos de la muerte,* which would soon become famous.

Mistral moved three times over the next three years to help reorganize troubled schools in different parts of the country. During this time she also passed certification exams qualifying her to teach at the secondary as well as the primary level, shoring up her tenuous livelihood. She made her first visit to the capital, Santiago, and took steps toward cultivating friendships with established writers there and abroad. In 1912 she sent an admiring letter and some poems to the Nicaraguan *modernista* Rubén Darío, who published them in his Paris magazine *Elegancias.* She developed a correspondence with Mexican poet Amado Nervo and by 1914 had established close relationships in the Chilean capital with Manuel Magallanes Moure and his friend Eduardo Barrios, who provided the editorial judgment the young writer needed to consolidate her work. They introduced her to the influential poet, architect, and businessman Pedro Prado and the artistic collective called Los Diez (The Ten). With Magallanes Moure the young poet later carried on an intense, almost completely epistolary romance in which she rehearsed all the emotions of an "impossible" love but carefully refused his requests to meet her alone in private.

Santiago in December 1914 was the site of the second annual Floral Games, a national civic celebration that culminated in a ceremony crowning a beauty queen and presenting the winners of a nationwide poetry competition. Magallanes Moure was one of three judges; he voted to award the grand prize to Mistral's *Sonetos de la muerte,* as did critic Armando Donoso, who had published Mistral's work in the periodical *Sucesos.* Mistral declined to appear onstage while her poems

---

10 Onlooker: Lucila Godoy to Manuel Magallanes Moure, 20 May 1915, in *Cartas,* 15–16. Rival: Carmen Conde quoted in Carlos Perozzo, "Gabriela Mistral," in *Forjadores del mundo contemporáneo* (Editorial Planeta, 1989), reprinted at www.letras .s5.com/biografiamistral2.htm.
11 "Suicidio," in *La Reforma* (La Serena), 26 November 1909, reprinted in *Recopilación,* ed. Zegers, 147–48.

were read or to receive the award in person; the reasons announced were the press of her teaching duties and her extreme humility. A story spread that she had watched from the balcony because she had no clothing suitable for the occasion.[12] The intensity of the sonnets, the poet's depiction as a humble teacher, and her tantalizing absence from the scene of her triumph all combined to create a memorable impression.

While Mistral's careers as a poet, intellectual, and public servant were yet to flower, the founding elements of a personal myth were already present. Childhood poverty, abandonment by her father, stigmatization as dull and useless, unfair barriers to formal schooling—all these things set her apart and formed a narrative of trials overcome, attesting to a kind of log-cabin authenticity in the popular imagination. A lurid romantic tragedy—evoked so vividly in the Sonnets of Death—that could be taken to explain the writer's choice of a solitary life, reinforced by her extravagant gesture of humility at the Floral Games and her deliberately austere and "unfeminine" manner and dress, also allowed the events of her early years to be read according to the template of the female saint's life. Indeed her first biography, written by Virgilio Figueroa when she was only forty-three, was titled *La divina Gabriela*.

As Mistral's pedagogical and literary writings gained international recognition, she herself became a moral symbol—as would, in their different ways, Anna Akhmatova and Václav Havel. As with these later figures, Mistral's symbolic weight was something to be recruited, opposed, or managed by powerful interests both during her life and after her death. Mistral was quite aware of this symbolism, of the "Saint Gabriela" myth, and often seems to have been complicit in its growth.

By 1917 Mistral had been teaching in the town of Los Andes for five years. She was earning some money from regular publications in periodicals, but her salary was small and fixed, and she agitated for a transfer as the only way to get a raise. Her poems had appeared in two anthologies, including one edited by Los Diez, and had become sufficiently well known to be objects of parody and factional controversy in Santiago.

About this time Mistral was introduced to local congressman Pedro

---

12 Perozzo, "Gabriela Mistral," www.letras.s5.com/biografiamistral2.htm.

Aguirre Cerda, who would become her most powerful ally and an eventual president of Chile. When in early 1918 he became minister of Justice and Public Instruction, he appointed her director of the *liceo* in the remote but politically important town of Punta Arenas on the Straits of Magellan.

Political Education: Punta Arenas, Temuco, Santiago

Mistral's self-styled "exile" in the Magallanes territory was brief but crucial. As unofficial ambassador from the Santiago government, the new director undertook morale-building activities, pressuring Santiago for resources and shaming local oligarchs to secure funding for library books and an expanded building. She kept Aguirre informed of labor unrest among the strongly anarcho-syndicalist workers, many of whom were immigrants, and of harsh responses by the military governor and wealthy landowning elite.

During this time she wrote or revised many of the poems that would be collected in her first book, *Desolación*. She also was writing on regular contract for the publisher Constancio Vigil in Buenos Aires, whose magazine *Atlántida* published her poetry and essays and whose company shared her interest in producing literature for children. The work supplemented her pay substantially, and Vigil's offer of a full-time position gave her a bargaining chip in her dealings with the educational bureaucracy.

Despite her accomplishments in Punta Arenas, Mistral found the cold almost unbearable and the conditions wearing. She continued to agitate for a transfer and in 1920 was sent to rainy, provincial Temuco, a town much less cosmopolitan than Punta Arenas but whose *liceo* was higher in the bureaucratic hierarchy, thus representing a promotion for its new director.

During her year in Temuco Mistral became friendly with the sixteen-year-old Neftalí Reyes Basoalto, soon to become known as Pablo Neruda. She encouraged the younger poet in his literary ambitions and later became an early advocate of his work abroad. In Temuco she also wrote and published the first version of the prose-poem sequence "Poemas de las madres," whose explicit portrayal of the physical and emotional experience of pregnancy and motherhood among the poor shocked many readers.

Mistral expanded her correspondence with writers, diplomats, and politicians from Mexico, Cuba, the Dominican Republic, and elsewhere. Spurred by the election of an old Santiago antagonist as senator for the Temuco district, and with the offer of work in Argentina in reserve, she began her campaign for an appointment as director of the capital's most prestigious *liceo* for girls—the best position to which a woman educator could aspire in Chile.

The national elections of 1920 had brought to power a coalition of Radicals, Liberals, and Democrats that represented a major gain for the progressive middle class over the old conservative elites. Many of Mistral's friends—Aguirre, Prado, and others—held positions of influence in the new government, and through their efforts and her own energies she received the appointment to the newly opened Liceo #6.

But again public controversy clouded her advancement. Her principal rival for the post, Josefina Dey del Castillo, was the wife of the secretary of the Radical Party's Central Committee. An insider, university educated, Dey complained in a newspaper about Mistral's lack of formal training, sparking a debate over professionalism and the relative strengths of the two women's credentials. Dey's husband was a Mason, and Mistral believed the Masons to be responsible for the campaign against her.[13]

Throughout her life Mistral was, in Leon Edel's memorable characterization of James Joyce, an injustice collector—chronically suspicious and pessimistic by nature.[14] The ministry supported her and sustained her appointment, but she felt injured and constrained by the resistance to it. As she thanked her supporters and took up the administration of the new school, she was already deciding to leave Chile.

Desolación, Mexico, and Exile

By 1922 Mistral's work was being published and esteemed throughout Latin America. In April her first book, *Desolación,* was printed in New York, having been solicited and sponsored by Federico de Onís, director of Columbia University's Instituto de las Españas. It would

13 Gabriela Mistral to Radomiro Tomic, 1952, in *Vuestra Gabriela,* ed. Vargas, 175–77.

14 "Perdonar es un don divino, o es una falta de dignidad" (Forgiveness is a divine gift, or it's a lack of dignity). Gabriela Mistral, quoted in Marta Elena Samatán, *Gabriela Mistral, campesina del valle de Elqui* (Buenos Aires: Instituto Amigos del Libro Argentino, 1969), 109.

go through two more editions within four years. The same month, Mistral revealed that she had been invited by the revolutionary Obregón government of Mexico to work with José Vasconcelos, who had been given wide powers to modernize the nation's educational system. A few months later she sailed for Mexico and a life of voluntary exile. Though she would retain complex official and private relationships with Chile throughout her life, she would never again live there.

Mistral brought with her the young sculptor Laura Rodig, who had worked as a teacher for her in Los Andes and had since served as her secretary and companion. Rodig was the first of several women on whom Mistral would rely throughout her life, personal assistants who helped with correspondence and domestic and administrative tasks. These women, who later included Palma Guillén, the Puerto Rican Consuelo "Coni" Saleva, and the American Doris Dana, were paid when Mistral could afford to do so, but they were also drawn by the travel and social opportunities the position offered, and by the poet herself. Mistral's dependence on them contributed to the myth of her saintlike unworldliness.

Mistral was met in Veracruz by Palma Guillén, a young professor sent by Vasconcelos to be her official companion while on assignment in Mexico. When they arrived in Mexico City, more than three thousand children were convened in Chapultepec Park to sing her poems in welcome. Already skilled at this kind of public theater, Mistral inaugurated an *escuela-hogar* ("school-home" for girls) named for her, where she received a standing ovation and was showered with flowers.[15]

Initially hired to help Vasconcelos establish libraries and a classic canon for citizenship on the North American model, Mistral instead joined his Rural Mission Project and traveled the countryside to instruct and inspire the pedagogues of the future. Mistral increasingly identified the nation (and later the region) with its children and saw its teachers as mothers in a kind of metaphoric national home. The name *escuela-hogar* given to residential schools enacted this symbolism—ironically, given that they removed students from

---

15 Diana Anhalt, "The Inconvenient Heroine: Gabriela Mistral in Mexico," in *Gabriela Mistral: The Audacious Traveler,* edited by Marjorie Agosín (Athens: Ohio University Press, 2003), 150–51.

their actual homes to enable them to shed their "barbarism" and acquire "civilization."[16]

In 1923 the ministry published an anthology of readings compiled by Mistral, to which she contributed original content, called *Lecturas para mujeres,* for use in schools. In its preface she declared, "*In my opinion, perfect patriotism in women is perfect motherhood*" (emphasis original). This claim of dignity for the traditional "women's sphere" and its importance for nation building would prove enduringly popular with readers despite its obvious vulnerability to feminist critique.

Nevertheless, Mistral was resented as an outsider by many in the Mexican educational establishment. By late 1924, Vasconcelos himself had resigned and a new presidential administration with other priorities had come to power. Mistral concluded her commitment and then spent the second half of the year traveling with Rodig in Europe, stopping en route to speak in Washington and New York. While in Spain she published her second volume of poetry, *Ternura,* containing lullabies, *rondas,* and other poems of childhood. She would later remove poems of this kind from *Desolación* and her third book, *Tala,* to include them in subsequent editions of *Ternura,* both to strengthen its thematic character and to signal a turn away from its emphasis on childhood.

Diplomacy and Parenthood

Returning briefly to Chile in 1925, Mistral retired after twenty years of educational service and started receiving a small pension. The following year, she began working for the Paris-based Institute for Intellectual Cooperation, an organ of the League of Nations similar to today's UNESCO. According to her later accounts, while she was staying in southern France a man claiming to be her half-brother appeared and entrusted her with his infant son, Juan Miguel Godoy (whom she called Yin-Yin), after the death of his birth mother.[17] She adopted the boy and raised him with the help of her friend Palma Guillén.

For the next two years Mistral traveled in France, Spain, and Italy.

---

16 Fiol-Matta, *Queer Mother,* 65–75.

17 Doris Dana, Mistral's literary executor and companion in her last years, told newspaper reporters in 2000 that Gabriela had "confessed" to her that Juan Miguel was her own natural son. Luis Vargas Saavedra presents reasons to be skeptical of this account in "Gabriela Mistral: Tía o madre de Yin Yin?" in the book review section of *El Mercurio* (Santiago), 20 November 1999.

Her own mother's death in July 1929 left her disconsolate. Then, at the end of that year, her pension—her only regular source of income—was suspended by a conservative Chilean administration as part of an austerity measure, reviving her lifelong anxiety about money. By 1930, of necessity, she had become a correspondent for most of the world's major Spanish-language newspapers; she traveled to New York to teach at Barnard College and taught at Vassar the following year. During these years of worldwide economic collapse, revolutions and coups occurred in Nicaragua, Brazil, Chile, and Argentina. The Spanish Republic was established in 1931 after the failure of Primo de Rivera's dictatorship.

In 1932 Mistral was named Chilean consul in Naples, but she resigned after three months when Mussolini's government refused her credentials on the grounds that she was a woman. The following year she made a lecture tour of Central America and held conferences on Hispanism in Puerto Rico. In 1934 she was appointed consul in Spain, a post that carried no salary apart from occasional commissions. Palma Guillén and Juan Miguel joined her in Madrid, where she continued to make her living from journalism. Later that year, following a petition by a distinguished group of European writers, a special act of the Chilean legislature made Mistral consul for life, with the right to choose her own residence (and, ironically, removing her from the normal ladder of promotion).

By 1935 Mistral was in Lisbon, having been forced to leave Madrid (where Neruda replaced her as consul) after a private letter critical of Spain was made public in Chile. Fascist organizations were growing in influence in Argentina and elsewhere in Latin America, though within six months after Franco launched the nationalist revolt in Spain in July 1936, Argentina and Mexico began accepting Spanish refugees. From Lisbon Mistral helped many republicans resettle across the Atlantic. In 1937 she participated in a Paris conference of intellectuals in support of the Spanish Republic, and the next year she visited Uruguay and Argentina, where her friend Victoria Ocampo's periodical *Sur* agreed to publish her third book of poetry, *Tala,* to benefit Spanish refugee children.

Later in 1938, Mistral's friend and early supporter Pedro Aguirre Cerda was elected president of Chile, heading a center-left coalition. Declining diplomatic appointments in Central America and Uruguay, Mistral, accompanied by her friend Coni Saleva, returned to southern France in early 1939. She settled in Nice, intending to work with refugees from the fall of the Spanish Republic in April.

Through this period of frequent movement, lecturing, journalism, and cultural diplomacy, Mistral repeatedly chose to reside in places—Madrid, Nice—that were full of intellectual ferment and directly in the political line of fire. Her assessments of conditions on the ground were valued by the numerous public figures among her wide circle of international correspondents, and she increasingly worried that her mail was being tampered with. When she sailed for France at the beginning of 1939, Hitler had already annexed Austria and the Munich Conference had made Germany's designs on Czechoslovakia clear. Shortly after her landing Prague fell, and by autumn France and its allies were at war with Germany. At the end of the year, the Ecuadorian writer Adela Velasco proposed to President Aguirre that Mistral be nominated for the Nobel Prize; Aguirre ordered the Chilean diplomatic service to see that her works were made available in several languages for the Swedish Academy.

War and Loss

Early in 1940, only weeks before the fall of France, Mistral along with Yin-Yin and Coni Saleva moved to Brazil. By May she had established a consulate in Niterói, across the bay from Rio de Janeiro. She soon moved to the old imperial city of Petrópolis, in a valley among the cooler hills to the east. In early 1942 she bought a house there, hoping Brazil would provide a haven from the European war and political storms in Chile. But a few weeks before she closed on the house, her Petrópolis friends, the Austrian writer Stefan Zweig and his wife Charlotte Altmann, committed suicide—an event that affected Mistral deeply. In Brazil, as in Buenos Aires and "neutral" Santiago, there were many who openly supported the Axis powers, and as consul Mistral was surrounded by people engaged in overt and covert intelligence activities.

During the nine months ending in May 1942, Mistral published versions of four poems that appear in this volume—"La dichosa," "La trocada," "La otra," and "La desasida"—in the Sunday edition of the Buenos Aires daily La Nación.[18] All reflect the upheaval she had expe-

---

18 "La dichosa," 12 October 1941; "La trocada," 15 February 1942; "La otra," 8 March 1942; "La desasida," 31 May 1942.

rienced and her struggle to find domestic peace while engaged with the "furious world." Then, in August 1943, Juan Miguel committed suicide by ingesting arsenic. He was seventeen. He died in a hospital with Mistral at his side, having left a brief suicide note that explained little. Mistral was physically and emotionally shattered. When she could write her friend Victoria Ocampo two months later, she was grasping for explanations.[19] Until the end of her life Mistral would tell different versions of the boy's death, but they all shared her belief that he had been taunted as an outsider by groups of his adolescent peers. As time went on she emphasized a xenophobic and racial aspect to the "gang" and its actions.[20] "I'm living on two planes, in a dangerous way," she wrote to Ocampo. In her grief, the poet claimed that Juan Miguel appeared to her and that she conversed with him.[21] She lived with a ghost and increasingly felt herself to be a ghost among the living. Around this time she developed symptoms of diabetes.

Triumph and Greek Tragedy

In 1945 Mistral became the first Nobel laureate in literature from Latin America. She traveled to Sweden to accept the award as "the direct voice of the poets of my race." On her return she visited England, newly liberated France and Italy, and Washington. By the end of 1946 she was living in Monrovia, outside Los Angeles, but she relocated the following year to Santa Barbara, where she bought a house. According to Margot Arce de Vázquez, many of the poems in her last collection, *Lagar,* were written there.[22] She participated in the 1946 founding of UNICEF.

In 1948 Mistral traveled to Mexico, where she lived in Veracruz and Jalapa. By 1949 she was soliciting a transfer to Italy, despite the Mexican government's encouragement to stay. By the end of 1950,

---

19 Gabriela Mistral to Victoria Ocampo, 26 October 1943, in *This America of Ours: The Letters of Gabriela Mistral and Victoria Ocampo,* edited and translated by Elizabeth Horan and Doris Meyer (Austin: University of Texas Press, 2003), 142–46.

20 "Y de leer vivo desde que me mataron a Yin los mulatos xenófobos de Brasil." (And I live from reading ever since the xenophobic mulattos of Brazil killed Yin on me.) Gabriela Mistral to Radomiro Tomic, 21 March 1950, in *Vuestra Gabriela,* ed. Vargas, 155.

21 Victoria Ocampo, "Victoria Ocampo on her Friendship with Gabriela Mistral," in *This America,* ed. Horan and Meyer, 316.

22 Margot Arce de Vázquez, *Gabriela Mistral: The Poet and Her Work,* translated by Helene Masslo Anderson (New York: New York University Press, 1964), 138.

she could write to a friend, "Yes, I have a book done: *Lagar*. . . . It will be done in Chile and they will distribute it very badly. But they have fabricated a story there that I'm ungrateful and I have to give them *Lagar*." [23]

Mistral was named consul to Italy in December 1950. She lived first in Rapallo and then Naples, again choosing European watering holes that served as cultural and political crossroads. At this time she was working on her long descriptive work *Poema de Chile*. Among her many excursions, she visited the Sibyl's grotto at Cumae and in 1952 was underlining her copy of Aeschylus: "I've been submerged *for two months* in Greek theater and there are now some notes on 'Electra' and 'Clytemnestra' and a bunch of others. This rereading, together with the Europe situation, has loaded me with pessimism and a su-permelancholy." [24] Mistral deplored the "bloc" of dictators that had emerged in South America and felt great anxiety about the prospect of another European war.

Mistral left Italy in 1953 and was named consul to the United States and general delegate to the United Nations by Chile's newly elected conservative-populist Ibañez government. She moved to Roslyn Harbor, New York, living in a house bought by her friend Doris Dana. Despite periods of ill health, she served on the UN Committee for the Rights of Women and traveled to Havana for the centennial celebrations of José Martí, an important influence on her thought and poetry.

In 1954 *Lagar,* her most complex and least "popular" book of po-ems, was published in Santiago. In September she made a month-long official visit to Chile—her first in decades—where she was met by enormous crowds at every stop. Returning to New York, Mistral continued work in the spring on *Poema de Chile,* but by this time her

---

23 "Sí tengo un libro hecho: *Lagar*. . . . Se hará en Chile y lo repartirán muy mal. Pero me han fabricado allá una leyenda de descastada y tengo que darles *Lagar*." Gabriela Mistral to Adelaida Velasco, December 1950 (published as 1948), in *Cartas*, 473.

24 Mistral's copy of Aeschylus (*Esquilo, la Orestíada* [Madrid: Compañía Ibero-americana de Publicaciones, n.d.]) bearing her underlining is now in the Gabriela Mistral Collection, Barnard College Library. "He estado sumergida, *por dos meses*, en el Teatro griego y hay ahora unos comentos de la 'Electra', la 'Clitemnestra' y otros bultos más. Esta lectura repasada junto a la situación Europa, me han cargado de pesimismo y de una super melancolía." Gabriela Mistral to Radomiro Tomic, 1952, in *Vuestra Gabriela,* ed. Vargas, 194.

health was clearly failing. She died of pancreatic cancer after a long hospitalization in Hempstead, Long Island, in January 1957. A requiem mass was celebrated in New York's St. Patrick's Cathedral, after which her body was repatriated to Chile for three days of national mourning.[25] Half a million people crowded the streets of Santiago to glimpse the body during an elaborate procession, wake, and state funeral. Her myth had finally triumphed, as she had foreseen during her visit in 1954: "I will wander the land of Chile like a phantom led by the hand of a child."[26]

MOTIFS AND TECHNIQUE

I believe in prophetic speech . . . still. I believe in Cassandra, I believe in Electra and in the charming Antigone. . . . For me, they're more alive than the [Institute for] Intellectual Cooperation and its choice group of old men.[27]

After Yin, my life is Lagar. *I write poetry because I can't disobey the impulse; it would be like blocking a spring that surges up in my throat. For a long time I've been the servant of the song that comes, that appears and can't be buried away. How to seal myself up now? . . . It no longer matters to me who receives what I submit. What I carry out is, in that respect, greater and deeper than I, I am merely the channel.*[28]

Mistral's *Locas mujeres* poems have been called self-portraits by many critics, notably Palma Guillén, who was better placed than most to recognize a likeness.[29] In an important sense they are; many describe

25 Marie-Lise Gazarian-Gautier, "Gabriela Mistral: La maestra de Elqui," in *Vida y obra,* vol. 4 of *Gabriela Mistral: Antología mayor* (Santiago: Cochrane, 1992), 105.

26 "Iré caminando por la tierra de Chile como un fantasma llevado de la mano por un niño." Magdalena Spínola, *Gabriela Mistral, huéspeda de honor de su patria* (Guatemala City: Talleres de la Tipografía Nacional, 1968), 32.

27 Gabriela Mistral to Victoria Ocampo, 29 May 1939, in *This America,* ed. Horan and Meyer, 99.

28 "Después de Yin, la vida mía es *Lagar.* Escribo poesía porque no puedo desobedecer el impulso, sería como cegar un manantial que pecha en la garganta. Hace tanto tiempo que soy la sierva del canto que viene, que acude y que no puede ser sepultado. ¿Cómo sellarme ahora? . . . Ya no me importa quiénes reciban lo que entrego. Cumplo por respeto a eso, más grande y profundo que yo, del cual soy el mero caño." Gabriela Mistral to Fedor Ganz, 4 January 1955, in *Cartas,* 574.

29 Palma Guillén de Nicolau, introduction to Gabriela Mistral, *Desolación—Ternura—Tala—Lagar,* 2nd ed. (Mexico City: Editorial Porrua, 1976), xxxvi.

with "meticulous clarity the spiritual states through which she was passing" after the death of her adopted son and the last of her relatives. Biography also illuminates private references and hermetic imagery in the poems. But Mistral saw herself as a witness, giving voice to the trials of a residence on earth—both her own and those of others.

At least four of the poems included here were written before Juan Miguel's suicide.[30] From 1939, when she invoked Cassandra to her friend Victoria Ocampo (who would herself be imprisoned under Juan Perón's regime), Mistral was pursued by history. As Margot Arce has noted, "During this period were World War II, the Korean War, the Cold War; denouncing was promoted and rewarded, persecutions, concentration camps, refinements of physical and psychological tortures; forced, mass exodus, insecurity, suspicion, fear, hysteria, thermonuclear bombs. Those years saw such an absolute undermining of values that peace became a 'cursed word,' and those who wanted peace became suspect and persecuted."[31] Mistral in these years was constantly on the move, and the doleful occasions for her endless departures left their marks on her poetry.

As a channel for "the song that comes," Mistral's medium was ventriloquy. In the dramatic monologues of the "madwomen," the poet plays the part of prophet or sibyl, speaking through the masks of personae. To the extent that they form a composite portrait, the poems imply a fragmented subject; as songs of experience, they question the possibility of a unitary subject—a *mujer* who is not *loca*—in the face of extreme conditions. Here, as in her earlier work, it is specifically the experience of women that exposes the costs of history and the madness of a calculus that accepts those costs.

Striking in these poems is the motif of wandering, displacement, and exile. Speakers walk, rest along the road, are carried off, slip away. The departures in Mistral's own life, often provoked by necessity, are only the most obvious of many sources for this imagery. The folklore of Mistral's childhood supplied vagabonds and ghosts to haunt the valleys of Norte Chico.[32] Both the Hebrew Scriptures

---

30 See note 18 above for titles and dates of first publication.
31 Arce, *Gabriela Mistral*, 61.
32 Graciela Illanes Adaro, *Gabriela Mistral y el valle de Elqui* (Santiago de Chile: Joaquín Almendros, 1971), 12–14, 30–32.

and Greek tragedy depicted prophets without honor in their own countries—a role with which she came to identify. Her complex spirituality included admiration for the mendicant St. Francis and his itinerant followers. Most immediate during the writing of these poems was the experience of involvement with refugees—among both her European intellectual circle and the people she assisted in her capacities as diplomat and volunteer.

The mirror images of wandering and exile are confinement and abandonment, topoi that also appear in *Locas mujeres*. From her early years in Punta Arenas, Mistral's public appearances and readings in prisons acknowledged their institutional similarities to schools and helped focus attention on the conditions of the inmates, some of whom were political prisoners. In Temuco's prison the inmates had greeted her with a "horrible music," clinking their chains as she passed—a sound that echoes in the image "little birds of perdition" from "Mujer de prisionero." In a poem like "La abandonada" Mistral was not only recapitulating family history but speaking for thousands of deserted women in northern Chile, and by extension across the globe. In this mode Mistral can usefully be compared to Akhmatova: " 'Can you describe this?' . . . 'I can.' " [33]

Confinement and abandonment can be psychic as well as physical. The madwomen of these poems are often trapped: the helpless Clytemnestra who must listen as a mob cheers the immolation of her daughter; the sleepless woman who can't escape the ghost that nightly climbs her stairs. A bereaved farm woman continues her pointless routines, abandoned even by death, while the ballerina liberates herself by sacrificing everything but cannot shake off the "red envenomed robe" of society's demands.

Sometimes wandering and entrapment meet in the same poem. The speaker of "La contadora" articulates the personal cost of witness, as the itinerant "servant of the song" becomes surrounded, overwhelmed, and exhausted by the burden of other people's stories. Here and in "La desasida" one senses Mistral's fear that her creative individuality had been eclipsed by her work as a spokesperson, that she had become but a shadow of her own myth. The tone of these

33 Anna Akhmatova, "Requiem 1935–1940," in *Poems of Akhmatova,* translated by Stanley Kunitz and Max Hayward (New York: Houghton Mifflin, 1973), 99.

poems contrasts sharply with that of her earlier, widely reprinted "Decálogo del artista" and "La oración de la maestra," which enjoin sacrifice and service.

Transgression and Transformation

The rubric *Locas mujeres* relates to a cluster of other terms that serve as titles and keywords both for series and for individual poems, beginning with Mistral's second book, *Ternura*, and becoming increasingly important over her career. The word *desvariar* (to rave) is one of these, evoking at once the divine madness of prophets and oracles, ecstatic intoxication, and the derangement of grief or suffering. Mistral had an early exemplar in her paternal grandmother, Isabel Villanueva, confined in old age to a single room and "constantly delirious." Other related terms are *alucinación* and several compounds with *loca* (*locas letanías, historias de loca*). All these terms function, as they do in *Locas mujeres*, to bracket, ironize, or disarm transgressive speech. From the mother who prays that her child not grow so that he won't age and die ("¡Que no crezca!" in the "La desvariadora" section of *Ternura*) to Clytemnestra's antiwar tirade, Cassandra's masochistic pledge of love, or Mistral's protestation against her own legend, this rhetorical ploy licenses readers to engage the forbidden and thus opens a space for cultural critique.

Hallucination, prophecy, and raving, as types of altered psychic states and radical idiosyncrasy, resemble dreams. Mistral sometimes uses the dream explicitly as a trope in *Locas mujeres,* for example in "La desasida," but it informs her practice throughout the series. She shares with the surrealists a fondness for images that shade one into another as in dreams. In "La otra," the "other" of the title is first characterized as a blazing cactus flower, albeit one that can walk; later the extended image pivots on a simile and the "other" metamorphoses into a hungry eagle—also fiery—for the rest of the poem.

To the extent that the surrealists based their technique on the idea of the psychoanalytic unconscious, Mistral seems not to have followed them. Influences on the transformations and dream-logic of her imagery include the shape-shifters of European and Elqui folklore, the visions of Isaiah and the other Hebrew prophets, and mystics including Teresa of Ávila and John of the Cross. Of her reading practice, she once wrote: "The point is to *store up images*—to enrich yourself with them—and to free yourself from reading hurriedly. . . .

This is, above all, an exercise for being a creator and not a reciter." [34] Her study of theosophy, both early and late in life, informed her sense that she lived on "two planes, dangerously," after the death of her adopted son.

Again and again in *Locas mujeres,* the landscape presents a timeless, liminal space in which the boundaries between physical and spiritual realms dissolve. Given that Mistral had spent years in cultural and political diplomacy during tumultuous events, strikingly few markers of contemporary civilization appear in the poems. The terrain is rural or wild: houses, villages, lighthouses, farm buildings are virtually interchangeable among settings in ancient Greece, the Elqui valley, or biblical Palestine. While characteristically Chilean terrain and flora appear, even the *pino de carrasco* (*Pinus halapensis*) is called by its Mediterranean name *pino de Alepo* (Aleppo pine) in "Una mujer." Such a stripped-down scene contributes to a sense of suspension, of synchronic rather than diachronic time, of the step that's always "about to land, that never does." Electra wanders lost in the coastal mist, Cassandra sees both past and future as she stands poised at the door to Clytemnestra's palace, and the speaker of "La que camina"

. . . grows solitary as a tree
or as a creek nobody knows,
walking thus between an end and a beginning
as if ageless or in a dream.

While it no doubt owes something to Mistral's turn toward classicism, the unchanging, visionary topography also facilitates personification, the most characteristic trope in the series. Abstractions become plants or animals; landscape and creatures take on anthropomorphic qualities. These transformations often have a symbol-generating function that parallels the structure of parable or fable. The patterns of folk legend, theosophist and Christian parable, and Buddhist morality tale were significant for Mistral, as was the panentheistic spirituality of Francis. [35] Evidence internal to the

---

34 "La cuestión es *almacenar imágenes*—enriquecerse de ellas—y librarse de leer corriendo. . . . Es ese, sobre todo, un ejercicio para ser un creador y no un recitador." Gabriela Mistral to Radomiro Tomic, 1951, in *Vuestra Gabriela,* ed. Vargas, 165.
35 On her first trip to Europe in 1924–25, Mistral made pilgrimages both to Assisi and to Ávila.

poems also implicates these genres: "Marta y María" expands one of Jesus's parables; in "La desvelada" and "La que camina," people who see wanderers are said to count them as "fábula(s)"; the speaker of "Madre bisoja" concludes:

> So it was when I was born
> and is, in the twilight of my day,
> and I tell, from what is known,
> what you might call a charade.

Poetics and Prosody

For all her own grief and disorientation during this period, Mistral remained a highly conscious artist, one whose poetics had changed decisively over time:

I was a scandalous romantic. *Desolación* scarcely floats on top of all that syrup. I learned later, from the classics and from life, not to burn as ostentatiously as the Ferias of Pamplona, in order to burn better; that is, with lasting coals, with hidden brands, like the eternal Greeks.

The whole vocabulary has to be different, either that of the bonfire or that of the brazier: instead of logs that soon go up in smoke, burning embers that throb slowly and smoothly. Nothing left over.

I look for primordial words that name truly, words without grime or wear, hard as the axles of hawthorn wood in the wagons of my Monte Grande.[36]

Like that of her fellow theosophist William Butler Yeats, Mistral's early style had emerged from nineteenth-century romanticism as a highly colored, self-consciously aesthetic manner, informed by regionalist ideas, folklore, and a heterodox spirituality. In Mistral's case, the French-influenced *modernismo* of the early Ruben Darío, the

---

36 "Fui una romántica escandalosa. *Desolación* flota apenas encima de tanto almíbar. Aprendí, después, de los clásicos y de la vida, a no arder tan aparatosamente como las Ferias de Pamplona, para arder mejor, es decir, con brasa larga, con tizón escondido, como los griegos de siempre.

"Todo el vocabulario ha de ser diferente, según la hoguera o según el brasero: en vez de los leños veloces en volverse humo, las pavesas que laten lento y suave. Nada les sobra.

"Busco palabras primordiales y que nombren derecho, palabras sin roña ni desgaste, duras como los ejes de madera de espino de mis carretas de Monte Grande." Gabriela Mistral to Fedor Ganz, 4 January 1955, in *Cartas,* 574–75.

regionalism of D'Annunzio and Frédéric Mistral, and the nostalgic pretensions of Spanish *cursilería* were formative.[37] "Perhaps those of my generation had the bad luck," she later wrote, "to leave the romantic lie only to come to the painted mask of the new school."[38]

With travel first to Mexico and then to Europe, Mistral increasingly felt the cultural currents that stirred in the aftermath of World War I. Direct social and political engagement, the democratization of art, the various utopian impulses around which international modernism would coalesce—these forces inevitably engaged her *campesino* populism and influenced her poetic practice. Her new vocabulary of "primordial words" paralleled the turn away from conventionally poetic diction that Yeats made in his middle period. Her journalism, pedagogical writing, and diplomatic service made her a public person, as Yeats the Irish senator would become a "sixty-year-old smiling public man."[39] When she turned again to personal events as a basis for poems, she did so with an enlarged human awareness—"I am a crowd, I am a lonely man, I am nothing," Yeats said—and the result was quite different from, and sometimes far more powerful than, anything she had produced before.

Mistral's search for elemental diction did not lead her—unlike her diplomatic colleague Neruda—to depart from traditional meter and rhyme. In this too her practice paralleled that of Yeats: "All that is personal soon rots; it must be packed in ice or salt. . . . Ancient salt is the best packing."[40] Mistral's insistence on "naming truly" and on striking imagery did, however, accompany a change in her relation-

<hr />

37 On the origins of the term *modernismo* in Latin America and Spain, see Matei Calinescu, *Five Faces of Modernity*, 2nd ed. (Durham, NC: Duke University Press, 1987), 69–78. For more on *cursilería*, see Noel Maureen Valis, *The Culture of Cursilería: Bad Taste, Kitsch, and Class in Modern Spain* (Durham, NC: Duke University Press, 2003).

38 "Tal vez los de mi generación tuvimos la mala fortuna de salir de la mentira romántica para pasar a la máscara pintada de la nueva escuela." Gabriela Mistral, "Extractos de una autobiografía," Gabriela Mistral Papers (microfilm), series 103, reel J, Library of Congress Manuscript Division, cited in Onilda A. Jiménez, *La crítica literaria en la obra de Gabriela Mistral* (Miami: Ediciones Universal, 1982), 152.

39 William Butler Yeats, "Among School Children," in *The Norton Anthology of Modern and Contemporary Poetry*, 3rd ed., vol. 1, *Modern Poetry*, edited by Jahan Ramazani, Richard Ellmann, and Robert O'Clair (New York: W. W. Norton, 2003), 124.

40 William Butler Yeats, "A General Introduction to My Work," in *Norton Anthology*, vol. 1, *Modern Poetry*, 886–87.

ship to form. As Tomás Navarro Tomás has observed, the characteristic *modernista* meters—*alejandrinos,* (fourteen syllables), *dodecasílabos* (twelve), and the dactylic modes of the *endecasílabo* (eleven) and *eneasílabo* (nine)—so abundant in her first book have virtually disappeared by the time of *Lagar.*[41] She tended to compose her later poems on a more restrained base of trochaic or polyrhythmic *eneasílabo, endecasílabo,* or *octosílabo* lines. Likewise she more often chose simple rhyme schemes of running or alternating *rima asonante,* and *Locas mujeres* includes several extended poems without rhyme.

Within this prosody of the brazier rather than the bonfire, Mistral was expressive and even innovative. She experimented with polyrhythmic lines of unusual stress patterns. More striking were her heterodox combinations of meters within a single poem, corresponding to emotional or semantic modulations in the work. As she became more comfortable with this technique, her polymetric interventions became more extensive. Navarro Tomás notes the mixtures of eight- and nine-syllable lines in the *romances* "La abandonada" and "Una piadosa"; in "La desvelada," built on a base of *eneasílabos,* interpolated lines of eight and ten syllables represent nearly a third of the whole.

"La otra" shows the method clearly. It opens with a two-line stanza composed of a divided decasyllable: five and five. The quatrains that follow are based on various combinations of octosyllables and heptasyllables, with their intimations of divided *alejandrinos.* Mistral strategically substitutes the shorter five-syllable line to mark a dramatic turn or create expressive closure—including, in the final stanza, an interlaced mirroring of the opening couplet.

In "Electra en la Niebla," a poem in unrhymed *endecasílabos,* Mistral inserts a single alexandrine at a critical juncture: *o yo me tumbe, para detenerte con mi cuerpo tu carrera* ("or take a fall, to stay your course with my body"). Clearly sound is here an echo to the sense—the extra three syllables of this line interrupt the metrical flow even as Electra imagines impeding her brother's journey.

Mistral also on occasion used imperfect or slant rhymes, violating canonical practice in a way analogous to that of the English trench poet Wilfred Owen, if far less systematically. Summarizing Mistral's prosodic practice, Navarro Tomás argues that "there is no reason to

---

41 Tomás Navarro Tomás, "Métrica y ritmo de Gabriela Mistral," in *Los poetas en sus versos: Desde Jorge Manrique a García Lorca* (Barcelona: Ediciones Ariel, 1973), 294.

think that these subtle movements and transitions in the structure of the poems were produced by mere and arbitrary chance. . . . Under the appearance of improvisation and carelessness, she cultivated a finely elaborated metric. She paid more attention to the musical power of the line than to its academic polish. She left abundant details of apparent indiscipline as a surprise for the rule-bound reader."[42] Margaret Bates observes in her introduction to Doris Dana's 1971 bilingual selection that in Mistral, as in "the great Spanish Symbolist poet Antonio Machado, the effect of utter simplicity is backed up by a subtle, complex, hidden machine that extracts from each word, from each sound and accent, its maximum emotional charge. This type of poetry, because of the complexity beneath the surface, is the least translatable." [43]

THE TRANSLATIONS

It is a critical commonplace that English speakers do not hear syllabics. That is, in a poem without a regular accentual meter, the ear will not perceive the regularity in a series of lines of unvarying syllable count. And yet, as Rodney Williamson says, "the task of the translator of Gabriela Mistral begins with a decision about the metrical and sonic structure of the text." [44] There are other challenges as well. English uses a primarily stress-based metrical system, and the odds of finding English rhyme words to approximate running *rima asonante,* for example, without doing violence to the sense are vanishingly small. And in the *Locas mujeres* poems, Mistral's rhythms are often constructed from a collage or quilt of metrical fragments rather than a uniform meter. In my versions I've invoked the concept of pattern density to address these issues, using the resources of the target language to sug-

---

42 "Ningún motivo hay para pensar que estos sutiles movimientos y transiciones en la estructura de los poemas se produjera por mero y arbitrario azar. . . . Bajo apariencia de improvisación y descuido, cultivó una métrica refinadamente elaborada. Atendió a la virtud musical del verso más que su pulimento académico. Dejó abundantes detalles de aparente indisciplina para sorpresa del lector preceptista." Ibid., 324–25.

43 Margaret Bates, introduction to *Selected Poems of Gabriela Mistral,* edited and translated by Doris Dana (Baltimore: Johns Hopkins University Press, 1971), xv.

44 Rodney Williamson, "Arte de disparidades y de confluencias: Reflexiones sobre la traducción de la poesía de Gabriela Mistral al ingles," in *Re-leer hoy a Gabriela Mistral: Mujer, historia y sociedad en América Latina,* edited by Gastón Lillo and J. Guillermo Renart (Ottawa: University of Ottawa, 1997), 162.

gest a comparable degree of order or disorder in the English as in the Spanish line—a similar ratio of pattern to variation.

To develop a rhythmic feel analogous to Mistral's Spanish, I have exploited speech stresses, a shared resource that can be manipulated more subtly in English than rhyme or fixed meter. Counting speech stresses (which exist in tension with those ordained by the metrical mode) in each Spanish line, I've noted where in the argument and emotional development of the poem the numbers varied, with an eye to attempting analogous effects. These include, for example, duplicating the initial and terminal stresses in the opening line of "La otra," which reinforce both its sense and its drama. Although using stress in this way somewhat exaggerates its importance in Spanish prosody, the strategy helps give a feeling of familiarity in the English that's rooted in the original. Likewise, though I have not preserved syllable counts precisely, I've tried to be alert to Mistral's line lengths and their modulations and to apply a similar purposefulness to the English versions, rather than allowing line lengths to vary arbitrarily to accommodate other needs. In retaining these metrical ghosts I am conscious of admitting, in a modest way, an emphasis of the source language perceptibly "foreignizing" to the target language—a practice theorized most cogently by Lawrence Venuti.[45]

The translator from a gendered language such as Spanish must evaluate how important the gender of a given substantive expression is to its meaning and poetic function. Is it mere convention, in which case an ungendered English word may be used alone, or does it represent an act of authorial specifying or emphasis that calls for the addition of clarifying English terms? Mistral's work, and particularly *Locas mujeres,* requires particular sensitivity on this point: often she clearly intends a female agent, sometimes in a nontraditional role; at other times she deliberately ambiguates the gender of a referent by using circumlocutions like "the one who" where convention would expect a person of specific gender. In the latter situation I have occasionally rendered a line more freely to avoid an awkward or prejudicial English construction. These few anomalies are itemized in the notes to the poems.

---

45 Lawrence Venuti, *The Translator's Invisibility: A History of Translation* (London: Routledge, 1995), 148–86.

Syntax and Diction

The syntactical peculiarities of Mistral's style in *Locas mujeres* pose their own challenges both to reader and translator. Her ambiguous use of reflexive and appositive structures, among others, contributes to what Arce calls the "characteristic trait of this poetic cosmos": its "fluidity, the fusion of boundaries until they are completely erased." [46] Like personification and anthropomorphism, syntactical ambiguity promotes identification across boundaries—those between animate and inanimate, abstract and concrete, subject and object. I've tried to preserve this quality wherever possible; where I've been forced to privilege one reading over another, I've chosen what seemed the more suggestive rather than the more reductive.

Another aspect of Mistral's syntactic practice is her penchant for compression, parallel grouping, and repetition. These most often serve musical and rhetorical ends. For example, in stanza three of "La otra," she collapses two parallel thoughts (*piedra tenía a pies* and *cielo tenía a espaldas*) into one clause by relating the pair of landscape elements to the pair of body parts via a single verb. This odd structure does not result from the inflected nature of Spanish; it's only marginally less idiosyncratic in the original than in English. Apart from adding pattern density by creating a pair of adjacent pairs, the construction allows the poet to pack three *ie* diphthongs in quick succession to striking musical effect. Here again I've endeavored to recognize these techniques and find English equivalents or analogues where possible.

Arce and others have noted the relative abundance in these poems of Latinisms, *cultismos* (words brought phonetically unchanged from classical languages), and phrases that echo biblical or liturgical formulas. The tonal and allusive importance for the translator of such elements should be obvious. Mistral also made skillful use of words with more than one unrelated meaning, in which a term's primary sense carries local meaning in the line while a secondary sense invokes a theme or motif. An example is the word *acedía* in line 2 of "La abandonada," whose primary meaning of "sourness" is part of an image characterizing the speaker's emotional state. Its second signification, the theological sin of sloth, hovers in the background and prompts the

---

46 Arce, *Gabriela Mistral,* 91.

reader to consider the moral quality of the speaker's actions. Where a corresponding polysemy is not available in a single English term, I have rendered the primary sense and glossed the word in the notes.

Mistral's choice of the adjective *grávidas* to describe fountains in "Clitemnestra," a poem spoken by a mother while her child burns, is clearly intended to invoke both the modern sense of "burgeoning" and the Latin root from which we still take the English term *gravid*, or pregnant. It's characteristic of Mistral's style to make unusual lexical choices in order to exploit such archaic or secondary meanings. The Old English form of *teem* means to give birth, bear offspring, or become pregnant and bears a relationship to its modern sense analogous to that of the Latin-Spanish pair. "Teeming" thus provides not only an accurate translation but also a way to render an aspect of Mistral's poetics. Such rare etymological correspondences are gifts to the translator.

Certain words reappear frequently in *Locas mujeres* as in Mistral's work generally. Some of these are simply favored diction, while others, like the tree-names she used for Juan Miguel, take on symbolic importance as recurring motifs. Another example is *ronda* (round), which is at once a children's ring-dance, the melody to which it is danced, and the verses set to that melody. Mistral wrote many *rondas* during her career, several of which are now among the most widely known poems in the language. In the context of *Locas mujeres,* the word's usage is complicated by Mistral's belief that Juan Miguel's circle of peers had tormented the boy to death. The range of connotation widens to include the sinister or demonic and touches on *ronda*'s alternate meaning of a patrol or company of watchmen. In translating this and other recurring words, I have not limited myself to a single English term consistently applied. Instead I've chosen what seemed the most semantically and sonically apt for each occurrence, knowing that in a bilingual edition the repeated Spanish words can be readily observed. This course has the further advantage of exposing a fuller range of meanings to the English reader over the span of the book and thus suggesting the depth of Mistral's "primordial" lexical practice.

From *Lagar* / W I N E P R E S S

LA OTRA

Una en mí maté:
yo no la amaba.

Era la flor llameando
del cactus de montaña;
era aridez y fuego;
nunca se refrescaba.

Piedra y cielo tenía
a pies y a espaldas
y no bajaba nunca
a buscar "ojos de agua".

Donde hacía su siesta,
las hierbas se enroscaban
de aliento de su boca
y brasa de su cara.

En rápidas resinas
se endurecía su habla,
por no caer en linda
presa soltada.

Doblarse no sabía
la planta de montaña,
y al costado de ella,
yo me doblaba . . .

La dejé que muriese,
robándole mi entraña.
Se acabó como el águila
que no es alimentada.

Sosegó el aletazo,
se dobló, lacia,
y me cayó a la mano
su pavesa acabada . . .

THE OTHER

I killed a woman in me:
one I did not love.

She was the blazing flower
of the mountain cactus;
05   she was drought and fire,
never cooling her body.

She had stone and sky
at her feet, at her shoulders,
and she never came down
10   to seek the water's eye.

Wherever she rested,
the grass would twist
from the breath of her mouth,
the live coals of her face.

15   Like quick-setting resin
her speech would harden,
never to fall lovely
as a captive freed.

The plant of the mountain
20   didn't know how to bend,
and at her side
I bent and bent . . .

I left her to die,
robbing her of my heart's blood.
25   She ended like an eagle
starved of its food.

The beating wing grew still;
she bent, spent,
and her dying ember
30   fell into my hand . . .

Por ella todavía
me gimen sus hermanas,
y las gredas de fuego
al pasar me desgarran.

Cruzando yo les digo:
—Buscad por las quebradas
y haced con las arcillas
otra águila abrasada.

Si no podéis, entonces,
¡ay!, olvidadla.
Yo la maté. ¡Vosotras
también matadla!

Still her sisters keen,
they cry to me for her,
and the fiery clay
rakes me as I pass.

35   When we meet I tell them:
"Search in the ravines
and fashion from the clay
another burning eagle.

"If you can't do it, then,
40   too bad! Forget her.
I killed her. You women
must kill her too!"

LA ABANDONADA

A Emma Godoy

Ahora voy a aprenderme
el país de la acedía,
y a desaprender tu amor
que era la sola lengua mía,
como río que olvidase
lecho, corriente y orillas.

¿Por qué trajiste tesoros
si el olvido no acarrearías?
Todo me sobra y yo me sobro
como traje de fiesta para fiesta no habida;
¡tanto, Dios mío, que me sobra
mi vida desde el primer día!

Denme ahora las palabras
que no me dio la nodriza.
Las balbucearé demente
de la sílaba a la sílaba:
palabra "expolio", palabra "nada",
y palabra "postrimería",
¡aunque se tuerzan en mi boca
como las víboras mordidas!

Me he sentado a mitad de la Tierra,
amor mío, a mitad de la vida,
a abrir mis venas y mi pecho,
a mondarme en granada viva,
y a romper la caoba roja
de mis huesos que te querían.

Estoy quemando lo que tuvimos:
los anchos muros, las altas vigas,
descuajando una por una
las doce puertas que abrías
y cegando a golpes de hacha
el aljibe de la alegría.

THE ABANDONED WOMAN

For Emma Godoy

Now I am going to learn
the sour country,
and unlearn your love
which was my only language,
05   like a river that forgets
its current, bed, and banks.

Why did you bring treasures
if you could pack no way to forget?
It's all left over and I'm left over
10   like a party dress for an unthrown party;
my whole life, I swear to God,
is left over from the first day!

Now give me the words
my wetnurse never gave me.
15   I'll babble them madly
from syllable to syllable;
the word "dross," the word "nothing"
and the word "waiting-for-death,"
though they coil in my mouth
20   like gaunt vipers.

I have sat down in the middle of the Earth,
my love, in the middle of my life,
to open my veins and my chest,
to peel my skin like a pomegranate,
25   and to break the red mahogany
of these bones that loved you.

I'm burning all that we had:
the wide walls, the high beams—
ripping out one by one
30   the twelve doors you opened
and closing with ax blows
the cistern of happiness.

Voy a esparcir, voleada,
la cosecha ayer cogida,
a vaciar odres de vino
y a soltar aves cautivas;
a romper como mi cuerpo
los miembros de la "masía"
y a medir con brazos altos
la parva de las cenizas.

¡Cómo duele, cómo cuesta,
cómo eran las cosas divinas,
y no quieren morir, y se quejan muriendo,
y abren sus entrañas vívidas!
Los leños entienden y hablan,
el vino empinándose mira,
y la banda de pájaros sube
torpe y rota como neblina.

Venga el viento, arda mi casa
mejor que bosque de resinas;
caigan rojos y sesgados
el molino y la torre madrina.
¡Mi noche, apurada del fuego,
mi pobre noche no llegue al día!

I'm going to send it flying,
the crop we gathered yesterday,
35   empty the skins of wine
and free the captive fowl;
I'll break like my body
the farmstead's pieces
and measure with raised arms
40   the harvest of ashes.

How it hurts, how it costs,
how divine things used to be—
they don't want to die, they resent dying,
and they open their bright guts!
45   The timbers reason and speak,
the wine stretches up to look,
and the flock of birds rises
ragged and slow as fog.

Let the wind come, let my house burn
50   better than a forest of resin;
let the mill and the braced tower
topple slantwise and red.
My night, hurried on by fire,
let my poor night not last till day!

LA ANSIOSA

Antes que él eche a andar, está quedado
el viento Norte, hay una luz enferma,
el camino blanquea en brazo muerto
y, sin gracia de amor, pesa la tierra.

Y cuando viene, lo sé por el aire
que me lo dice, alácrito y agudo;
y abre mi grito en la venteada un tubo
que la mima y le cela los cabellos,
y le guarda los ojos del pedrisco.

Vilano o junco ebrio parecía;
apenas era y ya no voltijea;
viene más puro que el disco lanzado,
más recto, más que el albatrós sediento,
y ahora ya la punta de mis brazos
afirman su cintura en la carrera . . .

Pero ya saben mi cuerpo y mi alma
que viene caminando por la raya
amoratada de mi largo grito,
sin enredarse en el fresno glorioso
ni relajarse en los bancos de arena.

¿Cómo no ha de llegar si me lo traen
los elementos a los que fui dada?
El agua me lo alumbra en los hondones,
el fuego me lo urge en el poniente
y el viento Norte aguija sus costados.

Mi grito vivo no se le relaja;
ciego y exacto lo alcanza en los riscos.
Avanza abriendo el matorral espeso
y al acercarse ya suelta su espalda,
libre lo deja y se apaga en mi puerta.

THE ANXIOUS WOMAN

Before he can start out, the north wind
sets in, there is a sickly light,
the road blanches like a dead arm and,
lacking love's grace, the land lies heavy.

05   And when he comes, I know by the gust
that tells me, lively and keen;
and my shout opens up a tube in the blast
that beguiles it, and covers his hair
and shields his eyes from the hail.

10   He seemed a thistledown or drunken reed,
was scarcely there, but he no longer whirls;
now he comes purer than a hurled discus,
straighter even than a thirsty albatross,
and now at last my outstretched arms
15   steady his waist on the way . . .

But already my body and my soul know
that he comes walking the livid
ribbon of my long shout, without
entangling himself in the glorious ash-tree
20   or relaxing on the sandbanks.

How could he not arrive, if the elements
I'm pledged to bring him to me?
The water lights him for me in the depths,
the fire hurries him to me in the sunset
25   and the north wind pricks his flanks.

My tireless shout doesn't loosen its grip;
blind and exact it finds him on the peaks.
It advances, parting the dense thicket,
and now as he nears it releases his back,
30   lets him go and fades away at my door.

Y ya no hay voz cuando cae a mis brazos
porque toda ella quedó consumida,
y este silencio es más fuerte que el grito
si así nos deja con los rostros blancos.

And there's no voice left when he falls in my arms
because it has all been used up,
and this silence is even stronger than the shout
if it leaves us like this, with our faces white.

LA BAILARINA

La bailarina ahora está danzando
la danza del perder cuanto tenía.
Deja caer todo lo que ella había,
padres y hermanos, huertos y campiñas,
el rumor de su río, los caminos,
el cuento de su hogar, su propio rostro
y su nombre, y los juegos de su infancia
como quien deja todo lo que tuvo
caer de cuello, de seno y de alma.

En el filo del día y el solsticio
baila riendo su cabal despojo.
Lo que avientan sus brazos es el mundo
que ama y detesta, que sonríe y mata,
la tierra puesta a vendimia de sangre
la noche de los hartos que no duermen
y la dentera del que no ha posada.

Sin nombre, raza ni credo, desnuda
de todo y de sí misma, da su entrega,
hermosa y pura, de pies voladores.
Sacudida como árbol y en el centro
de la tornada, vuelta testimonio.

No está danzando el vuelo de albatroses
salpicados de sal y juegos de olas;
tampoco el alzamiento y la derrota
de los cañaverales fustigados.
Tampoco el viento agitador de velas,
ni la sonrisa de las altas hierbas.

El nombre no le den de su bautismo.
Se soltó de su casta y de su carne
sumió la canturía de su sangre
y la balada de su adolescencia.

THE BALLERINA

Now the ballerina's dancing
the dance of losing everything.
She lets go of all she once had,
parents and siblings, fields and gardens,
05   the murmur of her river, the roads,
the tale of her home, her own face
and name, the games of her childhood,
as if to let everything fall
from her neck, her breast, and her soul.

10   At the break of the day and the solstice
she dances, laughing perfect dispossession.
What her arms fan away is the world
that loves and detests, that smiles and kills—
the land put to a vintage of blood,
15   the night of the glutted who don't sleep
and the shiver of a homeless man.

Without name, or race, or creed, stripped
of it all and of her self, she surrenders,
beautiful and pure, on flying feet.
20   Shaken like a tree and in the midst
of her turning, she's turned witness.

She's not dancing the flight of albatrosses
stippled with salt and the play of waves;
nor the uprising and defeat
25   of the beaten canefields.
Nor the wind, shaker of sails,
nor the smile of the tall grass.

They can't use her baptismal name.
She broke free of her clan and her flesh,
30   received the chalice-song of her blood
and the ballad of her adolescence.

Sin saberlo le echamos nuestras vidas
como una roja veste envenenada
y baila así mordida de serpientes
que alácritas y libres la repechan,
y la dejan caer en estandarte
vencido o en guirnalda hecha pedazos.

Sonámbula, mudada en lo que odia,
sigue danzando sin saberse ajena
sus muecas aventando y recogiendo
jadeadora de nuestro jadeo,
cortando el aire que no la refresca
única y torbellino, vil y pura.

Somos nosotros su jadeado pecho,
su palidez exangüe, el loco grito
tirado hacia el poniente y el levante
la roja calentura de sus venas,
el olvido del Dios de sus infancias.

Unknowing we throw our lives on her
like a red envenomed robe
and so she dances, struck by snakes
35   that free and eager climb her,
then let her fall like a conquered flag
or a garland torn to pieces.

Sleepwalker, changed into what she hates,
she keeps dancing, not knowing herself strange,
40   her grimaces puffing and drawing in,
she who pants with our panting,
cutting the air that never cools her,
solitary whirlwind, vile and pure.

We are ourselves her panting breast,
45   her bloodless pallor, the mad shout
thrown out to the west and the east,
the red fever of her veins, the neglect
of the God of her childhood days.

LA DESASIDA

En el sueño yo no tenía
padre ni madre, gozos ni duelos,
no era mío ni el tesoro
que he de velar hasta el alba,
edad ni nombre llevaba,
ni mi triunfo ni mi derrota.

Mi enemigo podía injuriarme
o negarme Pedro, mi amigo,
que de haber ido tan lejos
no me alcanzaban las flechas:
para la mujer dormida
lo mismo daba este mundo
que los otros no nacidos . . .

Donde estuve nada dolía:
estaciones, sol ni lunas,
no punzaban ni la sangre
ni el cardenillo del Tiempo;
ni los altos silos subían
ni rondaba el hambre los silos.
Y yo decía como ebria:
"¡Patria mía, Patria, la Patria!"

Pero un hilo tibio retuve,
—pobre mujer—en la boca,
vilano que iba y venía
por la nonada del soplo,
no más que un hilo de araña
o que un repunte de arenas.

Pude no volver y he vuelto.
De nuevo hay muro a mi espalda,
y he de oír y responder
y, voceando pregones,
ser otra vez buhonera.

THE WOMAN UNBURDENED

In the dream I had no father
or mother, joys or sorrows,
not even the treasure I have
to guard until daybreak was mine.
05   I bore no age or name,
neither my triumph nor my defeat.

My enemy could wound me
or my friend Peter deny me,
for I had gone so far
10   that no arrows reached me:
to a woman asleep
this world meant no more
than the other worlds unborn . . .

Where I was, nothing hurt:
15   neither seasons, sun nor moons
could sting me, neither blood
nor the verdigris of time;
no tall silos rose,
nor did hunger march around them.
20   And like a drunk I declared:
"My country, Fatherland, *la Patria!*"

But—poor woman—one
tepid thread clung to my mouth,
thistledown that came and went
25   with each trifling of the breath,
no more than a spider's silk
or a tide line on the sand.

I could have not returned, and I've returned.
Again there's a wall at my shoulder
30   and I must hear and answer
and, bawling street-cries,
be once more the peddler.

Tengo mi cubo de piedra
y el puñado de herramientas.
Mi voluntad la recojo
como ropa abandonada,
desperezo mi costumbre
y otra vez retomo el mundo.

Pero me iré cualquier día
sin llantos y sin abrazos,
barca que parte de noche
sin que la sigan las otras,
la ojeen los faros rojos
ni se la oigan sus costas . . .

I have my block of stone
and my handful of chisels.
35   I gather up my will
like abandoned clothes,
shake old habits from their sleep
and once more take up the world.

But someday I will go
40   with no tears and no embraces,
a ship that sails by night
without the others following her,
or the red beacons eying her,
or her own shores hearing her . . .

LA DESVELADA

En cuanto engruesa la noche
y lo erguido se recuesta,
y se endereza lo rendido,
le oigo subir las escaleras.
Nada importa que no le oigan
y solamente yo lo sienta.
¡A qué había de escucharlo
el desvelo de otra sierva!

En un aliento mío sube
y yo padezco hasta que llega
—cascada loca que su destino
una vez baja y otras repecha
y loco espino calenturiento
castañeteando contra mi puerta—.

No me alzo, no abro los ojos,
y sigo su forma entera.
Un instante, como precitos,
bajo la noche tenemos tregua;
pero le oigo bajar de nuevo
como en una marea eterna.

El va y viene toda la noche
dádiva absurda, dada y devuelta,
medusa en olas levantada
que ya se ve, que ya se acerca.
Desde mi lecho yo lo ayudo
con el aliento que me queda,
porque no busque tanteando
y se haga daño en las tinieblas.

Los peldaños de sordo leño
como cristales me resuenan.
Yo sé en cuáles se descansa,
y se interroga, y se contesta.
Oigo donde los leños fieles,

THE SLEEPLESS WOMAN

When the night thickens
and what is upright reclines,
and what is ruined rises up,
I hear him climb the stairs.
05   No matter that they don't hear him
and I'm the only one to sense it.
Why should another servant
in her vigil have to listen to it!

In one breath of mine he climbs
10   and I suffer until he arrives—
a mad cascade that his fate
sometimes descends and others scales
and a crazy feverish thorn
castanetting against my door.

15   I don't rise, I don't open my eyes,
yet I follow his shape complete.
One moment, like the damned,
we have respite beneath the night;
but I hear him go down again
20   as on an eternal tide.

All night he comes and goes—
absurd gift, given and returned,
a medusa lifted on the waves
that you see when you get close.
25   From my bed I help him
with what breath is left me
so that he won't hunt groping
and hurt himself in the darkness.

The stairtreads of mute wood
30   ring out to me like crystal.
I know which ones he rests on,
and questions himself, and answers.
I hear where the faithful boards,

igual que mi alma, se le quejan,
y sé el paso maduro y último
que iba a llegar y nunca llega . . .

Mi casa padece su cuerpo
como llama que la retuesta.
Siento el calor que da su cara
—ladrillo ardiendo—contra mi puerta.
Pruebo una dicha que no sabía:
sufro de viva, muero de alerta,
¡y en este trance de agonía
se van mis fuerzas con sus fuerzas!

Al otro día repaso en vano
con mis mejillas y mi lengua,
rastreando la empañadura
en el espejo de la escalera.
Y unas horas sosiega mi alma
hasta que cae la noche ciega.

El vagabundo que lo cruza
como fábula me lo cuenta.
Apenas él lleva su carne,
apenas es de tanto que era,
y la mirada de sus ojos
una vez hiela y otras quema.

No le interrogue quien lo cruce;
solo le digan que no vuelva,
que no repeche su memoria,
para que él duerma y que yo duerma.
Mate el nombre que como viento
en sus rutas turbillonea
¡y no vea la puerta mía,
recta y roja como una hoguera!

like my soul, complain to him,
35 and I know the ripe and final step,
about to land, that never does . . .

My house endures his body
like a flame that twists around it.
I feel the heat from his face
40 —a glowing brick—against my door.
I taste a bliss I never knew:
I suffer from living, I die of watching,
and at this tormented moment
my strength departs with his!

45 The next day I rehearse in vain
with my cheeks and my tongue,
tracing the blanket of haze
on the mirror in the stairwell.
And it calms my soul a few hours
50 until blind night falls.

The vagabond who meets him
makes the tale into a fable.
He scarcely carries flesh,
is hardly what he was,
55 and a look from his eyes
freezes some and others burns.

Let none question him who meet him;
just tell him not to return,
tell his memory not to climb
60 so he can sleep and I can sleep.
Destroy the name that storms
like a whirlwind in its path,
and let him not see my door,
tall and red as a bonfire!

LA DICHOSA
A Paulita Brook

Nos tenemos por la gracia
de haberlo dejado todo;
ahora vivimos libres
del tiempo de ojos celosos;
y a la luz le parecemos
algodón del mismo copo.

El Universo trocamos
por un muro y un coloquio.
País tuvimos y gentes
y unos pesados tesoros,
y todo lo dio el amor
loco y ebrio de despojo.

Quiso el amor soledades
como el lobo silencioso.
Se vino a cavar su casa
en el valle más angosto
y la huella le seguimos
sin demandarle retorno . . .

Para ser cabal y justa
como es en la copa el sorbo,
y no robarle el instante,
y no malgastarle el soplo,
me perdí en la casa tuya
como la espada en el forro.

Nos sobran todas las cosas
que teníamos por gozos:
los labrantíos, las costas,
las anchas dunas de hinojos.
El asombro del amor
acabó con los asombros.

THE HAPPY WOMAN
For Paulita Brook

We have each other by the grace
of having abandoned everything;
now we live free from
the time of jealous eyes;
05   and in the light we seem
cotton of the same spinning.

We trade the universe
for a wall and a conversation.
We had a country and people
10   and a few heavy treasures,
and love, crazy and drunk
with plunder, gave it all away.

Love loved solitudes
like the silent wolf.
15   He came to dig his house
in the narrowest valley
and we followed his track
without asking to return . . .

To be precise and exact
20   as the sip fits the glass,
and not rob him of the moment,
and not waste his breath,
I lost myself in your house
like a sword in its sheath.

25   We don't need all the things
that used to give us pleasure:
the grainfields, the shores,
the wide dunes of samphire.
The wonder of love
30   has banished wonders.

Nuestra dicha se parece
al panal que cela su oro;
pesa en el pecho la miel
de su peso capitoso,
y ligera voy, o grave,
y me sé y me desconozco.

Ya ni recuerdo cómo era
cuando viví con los otros.
Quemé toda mi memoria
como hogar menesteroso.
Los tejados de mi aldea
si vuelvo, no los conozco,
y el hermano de mis leches
no me conoce tampoco.

Y no quiero que me hallen
donde me escondí de todos;
antes hallen en el hielo
el rastro huido del oso.
El muro es negro de tiempo
el liquen del umbral, sordo,
y se cansa quien nos llame
por el nombre de nosotros.

Atravesaré de muerta
el patio de hongos morosos.
El me cargará en sus brazos
en chopo talado y mondo.
Yo miraré todavía
el remate de sus hombros.
La aldea que no me vio
me verá cruzar sin rostro,
y solo me tendrá el polvo
volador, que no es esposo.

Our happiness is like
the honeycomb that hides its gold;
the honey with its heady weight
weighs on my breast,
35 and I go giddy, or grave,
I know and I don't know myself.

I no longer recall how it was
when I lived with the others.
I burned all my memory
40 like a hungry fireplace.
If I go back, I don't know
the tile roofs of my village,
and my foster brother
doesn't recognize me either.

45 And I don't want them to find me
where I've hidden from them all;
let them first find in the ice
the bear's escape hole.
The wall is black with time,
50 the lichen on the threshold, deaf,
and anyone who calls us
by our name soon tires.

In death I will cross
the court of creeping fungus.
55 He will bear me in his arms
like a felled, stripped poplar.
Still I will look upon
the crown of his shoulders.
The village that didn't see me
60 will see me pass faceless
and only the flying dust
will have me, who is no husband.

LA FERVOROSA

En todos los lugares he encendido
con mi brazo y mi aliento el viejo fuego;
en toda tierra me vieron velando
el faisán que cayó desde los cielos,
y tengo ciencia de hacer la nidada
de las brasas juntando sus polluelos.

Dulce es callando en tendido rescoldo,
tierno cuando en pajuelas lo comienzo.
Malicias sé para soplar sus chispas
hasta que él sube en alocados miembros.
Costó, sin viento, prenderlo, atizarlo:
era o el humo o el chisporroteo;
pero ya sube en cerrada columna
recta, viva, leal y en gran silencio.

No hay gacela que salte los torrentes
y el carrascal como mi loco ciervo;
en redes, peces de oro no brincaron
con rojez de cardumen tan violento.
He cantado y bailado en torno suyo
con reyes, versolaris y cabreros,
y cuando en sus pavesas él moría
yo le supe arrojar mi propio cuerpo.

Cruzarían los hombres con antorchas
mi aldea, cuando fue mi nacimiento
o mi madre se iría por las cuestas
encendiendo las matas por el cuello.
Espino, algarrobillo y zarza negra,
sobre mi único Valle están ardiendo,
soltando sus torcidas salamandras,
aventando fragancias cerro a cerro.

Mi vieja antorcha, mi jadeada antorcha
va despertando majadas y oteros;
a nadie ciega y va dejando atrás

THE FERVENT WOMAN

In every place, with my arm and my breath,
I have kindled the old fire;
in every land they've seen me tending
the pheasant that fell from heaven,
05 and I know ways to make the nest
gathering its chicks from the coals.

It's gentle lulling in spread embers,
tender when I start it in little straws.
I know tricks to fan its sparks
10 until it rises with manic limbs.
It was hard, without wind, to light and stir it:
it was either smoke or hissing;
but now like a solid column it rises
upright, strong, faithful, in great silence.

15 There's no gazelle that leaps the torrents
and scrub-oak thickets like my mad deer;
in nets, no golden fish have thrashed
with such wild redness from their shoal.
I've sung and danced around its ring
20 with rhymers, kings, and goatherds,
and when it was dying into cinders
I learned to stoke it with my own body.

Men must have crossed my village
with torches the night I was born,
25 or my mother roamed over the slopes
igniting the clumps of brush.
Hawthorn, mesquite, and blackberry
are blazing across my matchless Valley,
unleashing their twisted salamanders,
30 fanning fragrances hill to hill.

My ancient torch, my trembling torch
goes waking the sheepfolds and hills;
it blinds no one and leaves behind

la noche abierta a rasgones bermejos.
La gracia pido de matarla antes
de que ella mate el Arcángel que llevo.

(Yo no sé si lo llevo o si él me lleva;
pero sé que me llamo su alimento,
y me sé que le sirvo y no le falto
y no lo doy a los titiriteros.)

Corro, echando a la hoguera cuanto es mío.
Porque todo lo di, ya nada llevo,
y caigo yo, pero él no me agoniza
y sé que hasta sin brazos lo sostengo.
O me lo salva alguno de los míos,
hostigando a la noche y su esperpento,
hasta el último hondón, para quemarla
en su cogollo más alto y señero.

Traje la llama desde la otra orilla,
de donde vine y adonde me vuelvo.
Allá nadie la atiza y ella crece
y va volando en albatrós bermejo.
He de volver a mi hornaza dejando
caer en su regazo el santo préstamo.

¡Padre, madre y hermana adelantados,
y mi Dios vivo que guarda a mis muertos:
corriendo voy por la canal abierta
de vuestra santa Maratón de fuego!

the night, stripped to vermilion rags.
35   I ask for the grace to kill that night
before she kills the Archangel I bear.

(I don't know if I bear him or he bears me;
but I know I call myself his food,
and I know I serve him without fail
40   and I don't give him to puppeteers.)

I run, throwing all that's mine on the bonfire.
Since I gave all, I carry nothing,
and I fall, but he doesn't pain me
and I bear him even at the cost of my arms.
45   Or one of my own saves him for me,
harrowing the night and her terrors
down to the lowest depths, to burn her
on the highest, most solitary peak.

I brought the flame from the other shore
50   where I came from and where I return.
There no one stirs it, yet it grows
and soars like a scarlet albatross.
I must return to my foundry and there
in its lap lay down the sacred loan.

55   Father, mother and sister gone ahead,
and my living God who keeps my dead:
I am running over the open course
of your holy marathon of fire!

LA FUGITIVA

Árbol de fiesta, brazos anchos,
cascada suelta, frescor vivo
a mi espalda despeñados:
¿quién os dijo de pararme
y silabear mi nombre?

Bajo un árbol yo tan solo
lavaba mis pies de marchas
con mi sombra como ruta
y con el polvo por saya.

¡Qué hermoso que echas tus ramas
y que abajas tu cabeza,
sin entender que no tengo
diez años para aprenderme
tu verde cruz que es sin sangre
y el disco de tu peana!

Atísbame, pino-cedro,
con tus ojos verticales,
y no muevas ni descuajes
los pies de tu terrón vivo:
que no pueden tus pies nuevos
con rasgones de los cactus
y encías de las risqueras.

Y hay como un desasosiego,
como un siseo que corre
desde el hervor del Zodíaco
a las hierbas erizadas.
Viva está toda la noche
de negaciones y afirmaciones,
las del Ángel que te manda
y el mío que con él lucha;

y un azoro de mujer
llora a su cedro de Líbano

THE FUGITIVE WOMAN

Festival tree, branches wide,
loose cascade, lively freshness
falling steeply at my back:
Who told you to stop me
05   and sound out my name?

Under a tree, I was only
washing the journeys from my feet
with my shadow for a road
and dust for a skirt.

10   How lovely that you throw out your limbs
and that you lower your head,
without grasping that I
don't have ten years to learn
your green cross that has no blood
15   and the disk of your pedestal!

Examine me, cedar-pine,
with your vertical eyes,
and don't move or uproot
your feet from the living soil:
20   your new feet can't take it
with scrapes from the cactuses
and bites from the cliffs.

There's a kind of restlessness,
like a hissing that runs
25   from the simmering zodiac
to the bristling grass.
The whole night is alive
with negations and affirmations,
those of the Angel who commands you
30   and mine who fights against him;

and a wreck of a woman
wails for her cedar of Lebanon

caído y cubierto de noche,
que va a marchar desde el alba
sin saber ruta ni polvo
y sin volver a ver más
su ronda de dos mil pinos.

¡Ay, árbol mío, insensato
entregado a la ventisca
a canícula y a bestia
al azar de la borrasca.
Pino errante sobre la Tierra!

fallen and covered by night,
who's going to leave at dawn
35   knowing neither road nor dust
and without ever seeing again
his circle of two thousand pines.

Oh, tree of mine, surrendered
senseless to the blizzard
40   to dog day and to beast
to the hazard of the tempest.
Pine wandering over the earth!

LA GRANJERA

Para nadie planta la lila
o poda las azaleas
y carga el agua para nadie
en baldes que la espejean.

Vuelta a uno que no da sombra
y sobrepasa su cabeza,
estira un helecho mojado
y a darlo y a hurtárselo juega.

Abre las rejas sin que llamen,
sin que entre nadie, las cierra
y se cansa para el sueño
que la toma, la suelta y la deja.

Desvíen el agua de la vertiente
que la halla gateando ciega,
espolvereen sal donde siembre,
entierren sus herramientas.

Háganla dormir, pónganla a dormir
como al armiño o la civeta.
Cuando duerma bajen su brazo
y avienten el sueño que sueña.

La muerte anda desvariada,
borracha camina la Tierra,
trueca rutas, tuerce dichas,
en la esfera tamborilea.

Viento y Arcángel de su nombre
trajeron hasta su puerta
la muerte de todos sus vivos
sin traer la muerte de ella.

THE FARM WOMAN

For nobody she plants lilac
or prunes the azaleas
and carries water for nobody
in her looking-glass pails.

05   Facing someone who gives no shade
though he's taller than her head,
she stretches out a damp fern
to play cat and mouse with.

She opens the gates though no one calls,
10   when no one comes in, she shuts them
and she tires herself for the dream
that takes her, frees her, and leaves her.

Turn aside the spring flood
that finds her crawling blind,
15   scatter salt where she sows,
bury her tools of iron.

Make her sleep; put her to sleep
like a civet or an ermine.
When she sleeps, lower her arm
20   and cast her dream to the wind.

Death wanders demented,
walks drunken about the earth,
he tangles roads, twists fates,
plays drumbeats on the globe.

25   Wind and Archangel, her namesakes,
delivered to her door
the death of all her loved ones
without delivering hers.

Las fichas vivas de los hombres
en la carrera le tintinean.
¡Trocaría, perdería
la pobre muerte de la granjera!

Bright gambling chips of mortals
30   jingle along his path.
He must have swapped, must have lost
the farm woman's poor death!

LA HUMILLADA

Un pobre amor humillado
arde en la casa que miro.
En el espacio del mundo,
lleno de duros prodigios,
existe y pena este amor,
como ninguno ofendido.

Se cansa cuanto camina,
cuanto alienta, cuanto es vivo,
y no se rinde ese fuego,
de clavos altos y fijos.

Junto con los otros sueños,
el sueño suyo Dios hizo
y ella no quiere dormir
de aquel sueño recibido.

La pobre llama demente
violento arde y no cansino,
sin tener el viento Oeste
sin alcanzar el marino,
y arde quieta, arde parada
aunque sea torbellino.

Mejor que caiga su casa
para que ella haga camino
y que marche hasta rodar
en el pastal o los trigos.

Ella su casa la da
como se entrega un carrizo;
da su canción dolorida,
da su mesa y sus vestidos.

Pero ella no da su pecho
ni el brazo al fuego extendido,
ni la oración que le nace

THE HUMBLED WOMAN

A poor humiliated love
burns in the house I see.
In the vastness of the world,
full of hard marvels,
05   this love exists and suffers,
wounded as no other.

Whatever walks tires,
whatever breathes or lives,
but it doesn't weary, this fire
10   of tall, unwavering spikes.

Along with the other dreams,
God made this dream of hers
and she doesn't want to sleep
as that dream's receiver.

15   The poor thing calls out madly
as it burns fierce and tireless,
even lacking the west wind,
even without the sea breeze,
yet it burns calm and still
20   in the face of a whirlwind.

Better if her house fell
so she'd take to the road
and walk until she tumbled
in pastures or wheatfields.

25   She gives up her house
as one surrenders a reed;
gives her sorrowful song,
gives her table and clothes.

But she doesn't give her breast
30   nor the arm held out to the fire,
nor the prayer born to her

como un hijo, con vagido,
ni el árbol de azufre y sangre
cada noche más crecido,
que ya la alcanza y la cubre
tomándola para él mismo!

like a child, with a wail,
nor the tree of sulfur and blood,
grown taller each night,
35 that now reaches and covers her
taking her for himself!

LA QUE CAMINA

Aquel mismo arenal, ella camina
siempre hasta cuando ya duermen los otros;
y aunque para dormir caiga por tierra
ese mismo arenal sueña y camina.
La misma ruta, la que lleva al Este
es la que toma aunque la llama el Norte,
y aunque la luz del sol le da diez rutas
y se las sabe, camina la Única.
Al pie del mismo espino se detiene
y con el ademán mismo lo toma
y lo sujeta porque es su destino.

La misma arruga de la tierra ardiente
la conduce, la abrasa y la obedece
y cuando cae de soles rendida
la vuelve a alzar para seguir con ella.
Sea que ella la viva o que la muera
en el ciego arenal que todo pierde,
de cuanto tuvo dado por la suerte
esa sola palabra ha recogido
y de ella vive y de la misma muere.

Igual palabra, igual, es la que dice
y es todo lo que tuvo y lo que lleva
y por su sola sílaba de fuego
ella puede vivir hasta que quiera.
Otras palabras aprender no quiso
y la que lleva es su propio sustento
a más sola que va más la repite,
pero no se la entienden sus caminos.

¿Cómo, si es tan pequeña, la alimenta?
¿Y cómo, si es tan breve, la sostiene,
y cómo, si es la misma, no la rinde,
y adónde va con ella hasta la muerte?
No le den soledad porque la mude,
ni palabra le den, que no responde.

SHE WHO WALKS

She always walks that same sand
until the others have gone to sleep;
and even though she drops in her tracks
she dreams and walks that same sand.
05   The same route, the one that leads east,
is what she takes though the north calls her,
and though daylight shows her ten routes,
and she knows them all, she walks the One.
She halts at the foot of the same thorn
10   and with the same attitude takes it
and she grasps it because it's her fate.

The same furrow in the burning earth
leads her, scorches and obeys her
and when she falters sun-struck
15   it lifts her again to go on with her.
Whether she lives or dies by it
on the blind sand where all is lost,
from everything fortune had given her
she has salvaged that single word
20   and she lives on it and dies of the same.

That self-same word is what she says,
it's all she kept and all she carries
and on its single syllable of fire
she can live as long as she wants.
25   She wanted to learn no other words
and the one she bears is her proper food;
the more alone she is, the more she repeats it,
but her roads don't understand.

How, if so small, does it feed her?
30   And how, if so brief, does it sustain her,
and why, if the same, doesn't it weary her,
and where is she taking it unto death?
Don't give her solitude hoping to change her,
don't say a word to her, she won't answer.

Ninguna más le dieron, en naciendo,
y como es su gemela no la deja.

¿Por qué la madre no le dio sino esta?
¿Y por qué cuando queda silenciosa
muda no está, que sigue balbuceándola?
Se va quedando sola como un árbol
o como arroyo de nadie sabido
así marchando entre un fin y un comienzo
y como sin edad o como en sueño.
Aquellos que la amaron no la encuentran,
el que la vio se la cuenta por fábula
y su lengua olvidó todos los nombres
y solo en su oración dice el del Único.

Yo que la cuento ignoro su camino
y su semblante de soles quemado,
no sé si la sombrean pino o cedro
ni en qué lengua ella mienta a los extraños.

Tanto quiso olvidar que ya ha olvidado.
Tanto quiso mudar que ya no es ella,
tantos bosques y ríos se ha cruzado
que al mar la llevan ya para perderla,
y cuando me la pienso, yo la tengo,
y le voy sin descanso recitando
la letanía de todos los nombres
que me aprendí, como ella vagabunda;
pero el Ángel oscuro nunca, nunca,
quiso que yo la cruce en los senderos.

Y tanto se la ignoran los caminos
que suelo comprender, con largo llanto,
que ya duerme del sueño fabuloso,
mar sin traición y monte sin repecho,
ni dicha ni dolor, no más olvido.

35   They gave her nothing else at birth,
     and since it's her twin, she won't leave it.

     Why did her mother give her only this?
     And why is it, when she keeps silent,
     that she's not mute but goes on babbling it?
40   She grows solitary as a tree
     or as a creek nobody knows,
     walking thus between an end and a beginning
     as if ageless or in a dream.
     Those who loved her don't meet her,
45   anyone who's seen her counts her a myth,
     and her tongue has forgotten all names
     and only in prayer speaks that of the One.

     I who tell of her don't know her path
     or her sunburned countenance,
50   I don't know if pine shades her or cedar,
     or in what tongue she names strangers.

     She wanted to forget so much that she's forgotten.
     She wanted to change so much she's no longer herself;
     she has crossed so many woods and rivers
55   that they've brought her to the sea to lose her,
     and when I think of her, I possess her,
     and for her I recite without rest
     the litany of all the names
     that I learned, like her a wanderer;
60   but the dark Angel never, never
     wanted my path to cross hers.

     And so little do the roads know of her
     that I've come to accept, with flowing tears,
     that she's gone to sleep the fabled sleep,
65   a sea without treachery and a peak without slope,
     no happiness or pain, no more forgetting.

MARTA Y MARÍA
Al doctor Cruz Coke

Nacieron juntas, vivían juntas,
comían juntas Marta y María.
Cerraban las mismas puertas,
al mismo aljibe bebían,
el mismo soto las miraba,
y la misma luz las vestía.

Sonaban las lozas de Marta,
borbolleaban su marmitas.
El gallinero hervía en tórtolas,
en gallos rojos y ave-frías,
y, saliendo y entrando, Marta
en plumazones se perdía.

Rasgaba el aire, gobernaba
alimentos y lencerías,
el lagar y las colmenas
y el minuto, la hora y el día . . .

Y a ella todo le voceaba
a grito herido por donde iba:
vajillas, puertas, cerrojos,
como a la oveja con esquila;
y a la otra se le callaban,
hilado llanto y Ave-Marías.

Mientras que en ángulo encalado,
sin alzar mano, aunque tejía,
María, en azul mayólica,
algo en el aire quieto hacía:
¿Qué era aquello que no se acababa,
ni era mudado ni le cundía?

MARTHA AND MARY

For Doctor Cruz Coke

Martha and Mary were born together,
lived together, ate together.
They closed the same doors,
drank from the same cistern.
05   The same grove watched them,
and the same light robed them.

Martha's dishes clinked,
her porridge-pot bubbled.
Her henyard teemed with doves,
10   with red cocks and plover.
Coming and going, Martha
was lost in a cloud of feathers.

In a whirlwind, she would rule
over meals and linens,
15   the winepress and beehives,
the minute, the hour and the day . . .

And wherever she went, all things
voiced a wounded cry to her:
crockery, latches, doors,
20   as to their bellwether;
and for her sister they grew hushed,
spinning tears and Ave Marías.

Meanwhile, in a whitewashed corner,
without lifting a hand, though she was weaving,
25   Mary, on blue majolica,
made something in the still air:
What was it that was never finished,
neither changed nor fulfilled?

Y un mediodía ojidorado,
cuando es que Marta rehacía
a diez manos la vieja Judea,
sin voz ni gesto *pasó* María.

Solo se hizo más dejada,
solo embebió sus mejillas,
y se quedó en santo y seña
de su espalda, en la cal fría,
un helecho tembloroso
una lenta estalactita,
y no más que un gran silencio
que rayo ni grito rompían.

Cuando Marta envejeció,
sosegaron horno y cocina;
la casa ganó su sueño,
quedó la escalera supina,
y en adormeciendo Marta,
y pasando de roja a salina,
fue a sentarse acurrucada
en el ángulo de María,
donde con pasmo y silencio
apenas su boca movía . . .

Hacia María pedía ir
y hacia ella se iba, se iba,
diciendo: "¡María!", solo eso,
y volviendo a decir: "¡Maria!"
Y con tanto fervor llamaba
que, sin saberlo, ella partía,
soltando la hebra del hálito
que su pecho no defendía.
Ya iba los aires subiendo,
ya "no era" y no lo sabía . . .

And one golden-eyed noon
30 when Martha with ten hands
was busy mending old Judea,
without word or sign, Mary *passed*.

She only grew more languid,
only drew in her cheeks,
35 and lingered as the countersign
of her shoulder on the cold lime,
a trembling fern,
a slow stalactite,
no more than a great silence
40 no lightning or cry would break.

When Martha grew old,
oven and kitchen rested;
the house gained its dream,
the ladder stayed unraised,
45 and on going to sleep Martha,
fading from ruddy to salt,
went to sit curled up
in that corner of Mary's,
where with wonder and silence
50 her mouth hardly moved . . .

She prayed to go to Mary
and she went and went toward her,
saying: "Mary!"—only that,
and saying again, "Mary!"
55 And she called out with such heat
that, without knowing, she departed,
releasing the thread of breath
that her breast didn't defend.
Already she was climbing the wind,
60 already *was not* and didn't know it . . .

UNA MUJER

Donde estaba su casa sigue
como si no hubiera ardido.
Habla solo la lengua de su alma
con los que cruzan, ninguna.

Cuando dice "pino de Alepo",
no dice árbol que dice un niño
y cuando dice "regato"
y "espejo de oro", dice lo mismo.

Cuando llega la noche cuenta
los tizones de su casa
o enderezada su frente
ve erguido su pino de Alepo.
(El día vive por su noche
y la noche por su milagro.)

En cada árbol endereza
al que acostaron en tierra
y en el fuego de su pecho
lo calienta, lo enrolla, lo estrecha.

A WOMAN

Where her house used to be she stays
as if it had never burned.
She speaks only her soul's words,
and to those who pass, none.

05 When she says "Aleppo pine"
she's not saying a tree but a child
and when she says "little stream"
or "golden mirror," she says the same.

When night falls she counts
10 the charred sticks of her house
or, lifting her brow,
sees her Aleppo pine stand tall.
(The day she lives for its night
and the night for its miracle.)

15 In every tree she raises
the one they laid in the ground,
and in the fire of her breast
she holds him, warms him, wraps him round.

MUJER DE PRISIONERO

A Victoria Kent

Yo tengo en esa hoguera de ladrillos,
yo tengo al hombre mío prisionero.
Por corredores de filos amargos
y en esta luz sesgada de murciélago,
tanteando como el buzo por la gruta,
voy caminando hasta que me lo encuentro,
y hallo a mi cebra pintada de burla
en los anillos de su befa envuelto.

Me lo han dejado, como a barco roto,
con anclas de metal en los pies tiernos;
le han esquilado como a la vicuña
su gloria azafranada de cabellos.
Pero su Ángel-Custodio anda la celda
y si nunca lo ven es que están ciegos.
Entró con él al hoyo de cisterna;
tomó los grillos como obedeciendo;
se alzó a coger el vestido de cobra,
y se quedó sin el aire del cielo.

El Ángel gira moliendo y moliendo
la harina densa del más denso sueño;
le borra el mar de zarcos oleajes,
le sumerge una casa y un viñedo,
y le esconde mi ardor de carne en llamas,
y su esencia, y el nombre que dieron.

En la celda, las olas de bochorno
y frío, de los dos, yo me las siento,
y trueque y turno que hacen y deshacen
de queja y queja los dos prisioneros
¡y su guardián nocturno ni ve ni oye
que dos espaldas son y dos lamentos!

Al rematar el pobre día nuestro,
hace el Ángel dormir al prisionero,

PRISONER'S WOMAN
For Victoria Kent

I have a man in that bonfire of brick,
I have my man, a prisoner.
Through bitter-edged corridors,
and in this slant bat-light,
05   groping like a diver in a grotto,
I walk on until I meet him,
and find my ridiculous painted zebra
wrapped in the rings of his mockery.

They've left him for me like a broken boat
10   with metal anchors on his tender feet;
they have sheared him like a vicuña
of the saffron glory of his hair.
But his Guardian Angel walks the cell
and if they never see him they're blind.
15   He came with him into the cistern pit;
took on the shackles as if submitting;
he stood to receive the cobra's clothes,
and stayed without heaven's air.

The Angel turns, milling and milling
20   the dense meal of the densest dream;
blots out his sea of blue-eyed waves,
drowns his house and his field of vines,
and hides the ardor of my burning flesh
and his essence, and his given name.

25   In the cell, the waves of stifling heat
and chill from the two—I feel them,
and each twist and turn that moan by moan
the two inmates make and unmake.
But the night guard neither sees nor hears
30   that two backs are there, and two laments!

At the close of this poor day of ours
the Angel makes the prisoner sleep—

dando y lloviendo olvido imponderable
a puñados de noche y de silencio.
Y yo desde mi casa que lo gime
hasta la suya, que es dedal ardiendo,
como quien no conoce otro camino,
en lanzadera viva voy y vengo,
y al fin se abren los muros y me dejan
pasar el hierro, la brea, el cemento . . .

En lo oscuro, mi amor que come moho
y telerañas, cuando es que yo llego,
entero ríe a lo blanquidorado;
a mi piel, a mi fruta y a mi cesto.
El canasto de frutas a hurtadillas
destapo, y uva a uva se lo entrego;
la sidra se la doy pausadamente,
porque el sorbo no mate a mi sediento,
y al moverse le siguen—pajarillos
de perdición—sus grillos cenicientos.

Vuestro hermano vivía con vosotros
hasta el día de cielo y umbral negro;
pero es hermano vuestro, mientras sea
la sal aguda y el agraz acedo,
hermano con su cifra y sin su cifra,
y libre o tanteando en su agujero,
y es bueno, sí, que hablemos de él, sentados
o caminando, y en vela o durmiendo,
si lo hemos de contar como una fábula
cuando nos haga responder su Dueño.

Cuando rueda la nieve los tejados
o a sus espaldas cae el aguacero,
mi calor con su hielo se pelea
en el pecho de mi hombre friolento:
él ríe, ríe a mi nombre y mi rostro
y al cesto ardiendo con que lo festejo,
¡y puedo, calentando sus rodillas,
contar como David todos sus huesos!

granting and raining unknowable blankness
in fistfuls of night and silence.
35 And from my house that keens for him
to his, which is a burning thimble,
I go and come, a living shuttle,
as if I knew no other course,
and at last the walls open and let me pass
40 through iron, tar, cement . . .

Whenever I arrive, my love
who eats mold and cobwebs in the dark
laughs out loud at the white and gold;
at my skin, my fruit, and my basket.
45 I uncover the hamper of fruit by stealth
and grape by grape I feed him;
I dole out the cider stingily
so a gulp won't kill my thirsty one.
And when he moves, his ashen chains—
50 little birds of perdition—follow.

Your brother lived with you all until
the day sky and threshold went dark;
but he is your brother, just as long
as salt is sharp and green wine sour,
55 brother with or without his number,
free or groping in his hole,
and yes, it's good that we speak of him,
seated or walking, awake or sleeping,
for we must tell him like a fable
60 when his Master calls us to answer.

When snow swirls over the rooftops
or a downpour soaks his shoulders,
my warmth contends against the ice
in the breast of my shivering man:
65 he laughs and laughs at my name and my face,
and the blazing basket with which I feast him,
and while I'm warming his knees I can,
like David, tell all his bones.

Pero por más que le allegue mi hálito
y le funda sus sangre pecho a pecho,
¡cómo con brazo arqueado de cuna
yo rompo cedro y pizarra de techos,
si en dos mil días los hombres sellaron
este panal cuya cera de infierno
más arde más, que aceites y resinas,
y que la pez, y arde mudo y sin tiempo!

But for all that my breath surrounds him
70   and his blood melts breast to breast,
how, with an arm bowed like a cradle,
can I burst the cedar and roof slates,
if men have sealed for two thousand days
this honeycomb whose hellish wax
75   burns more than oils or resins, more
than pitch—and burns mute and endless!

UNA PIADOSA

Quiero ver al hombre del faro,
quiero ir a la peña del risco,
probar en su boca la ola,
ver en sus ojos el abismo.
Yo quiero alcanzar, si vive,
al viejo salobre y salino.

Dicen que sólo mira al Este
—emparedado que está vivo—
y quiero, cortando sus olas
que me mire en vez del abismo.

Todo se sabe de la noche
que ahora es mi lecho y camino:
sabe resacas, pulpos, esponjas,
sabe un grito que mata el sentido.

Está escupido de marea
su pecho fiel y con castigo,
está silbado de gaviotas
y tan albo como el herido
¡y de inmóvil, y mudo y ausente,
ya no parece ni nacido!

Pero voy a la torre del faro,
subiéndome ruta de filos
por el hombre que va a contarme
lo terrestre y lo divino,
y en brazo y brazo le llevo
jarro de leche, sorbo de vino . . .

Y él sigue escuchando mares
que no aman sino a sí mismos.
Pero tal vez ya nada escuche,
de haber parado en sal y olvido.

A PIOUS WOMAN

I want to see the man of the lighthouse,
I want to go to the rocky point,
taste the wave in his mouth,
see the abyss in his eyes.
05   I want to reach him, if he's living,
old man of salt and brine.

They say he looks only eastward
—walled up while still alive—
I want to cut him off from his waves
10   so in place of the abyss he'll see me.

He knows all about the night
that's now my bed and my road:
knows undertows, octopus, sponges,
knows a cry that ends all knowing.

15   His faithful, battered chest
is spat on by the tides,
he's whistled at by gulls
and white as any wound,
and so still, so mute and absent,
20   he seems as yet unborn.

But I go to the lighthouse tower,
climbing the knife-edged track,
for the man who's going to tell me
the earthly and the divine.
25   One in each arm, I bring him
a jug of milk, a sip of wine . . .

And he keeps listening to seas
that love nothing but themselves.
But maybe now he listens to nothing,
30   stalled in forgetfulness and salt.

From *Lagar II*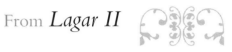

ANTÍGONA

Me conocía el Ágora, la fuente
Dircea y hasta el mismo olivo sacro,
no la ruta de polvo y de pedrisco
ni el cielo helado que muerde la nuca
y befa el rostro de los perseguidos.

Y ahora el viento que huele a pesebres,
a sudor y a resuello de ganados,
es el amante que bate mi cuello
y ofende mis espaldas con su grito.

Iban en el estío a desposarme,
iba mi pecho a amamantar gemelos
como Cástor y Pólux, y mi carne
iba a entrar en el templo triplicada
y a dar al dios los himnos y la ofrenda.
Yo era Antígona, brote de Edipo,
y Edipo era la gloria de la Grecia.

Caminamos los tres: el blanquecino
y una caña cascada que lo afirma
por apartarle el alacrán . . . la víbora,
y el filudo pedrisco por cubrirle
los gestos de las rocas malhadadas.

Viejo Rey, donde ya no puedas háblame.
Voy a acabar por despojarte un pino
y hacerte lecho de esas hierbas locas.
Olvida, olvida, olvida, Padre y Rey:
los dioses dan, como flores mellizas,
poder y ruina, memoria y olvido.
Si no logras dormir, puedo cargarte
el cuerpo nuevo que llevas ahora
y parece de infante malhadado.
Duerme, sí, duerme, duerme, duerme, viejo Edipo,
y no cobres el día ni la noche.

ANTIGONE

Once I knew the Agora, the Dircean
spring and the sacred olive itself,
not the road of dust and gravel
nor the frozen sky that bites the nape
05   and taunts the face of the hunted.

And now the wind that smells of mangers,
of sweat and the snorting of cattle,
is the lover that lashes my neck
and injures my back with his wail.

10   In summer they were going to marry me,
my breast was going to suckle twins
like Castor and Pollux, and my tripled
flesh was going to enter the temple
and give hymns and offerings to the god.
15   I was Antigone, scion of Oedipus,
and Oedipus was the glory of Greece.

The three of us walk: the white-haired man
and a battered cane that braces him
to push aside the scorpion . . . the viper,
20   and the sharp stone, and to shield him
from the faces of the wretched rocks.

Speak to me, Old King, where you can't go on.
I'm going to end up stripping you a pine
and making you a bed of these strange herbs.
25   Forget, forget, forget, Father and King:
the gods give, like twin flowers,
power and ruin, memory and oblivion.
If you can't go to sleep, I can carry
the new body that you now wear
30   like that of an ill-fated infant.
Sleep, yes, sleep, sleep, sleep, old Oedipus,
and reclaim neither day nor night.

LA CABELLUDA

Y vimos madurar violenta
a la vestida, a la tapada
y vestida de cabellera.
Y la amamos y la seguimos
y por amada se la cuenta.

A la niña cabelluda
la volaban toda entera
sus madejas desatentadas
como el pasto de las praderas.

Pena de ojos asombrados,
pena de boca y risa abierta.
Por cabellos de bocanada,
de altos mástiles y de banderas.
Rostro ni voz ni edad tenía
sólo pulsos de llama violenta,
ardiendo recta o rastreando
como la zarza calenturienta.

En el abrazo nos miraba
y nos paraba de la sorpresa
el corazón. Cruzando el llano
a más viento más se crecía
la tentación de sofocar
o de abajar tamaña hoguera.

Y si ocurría que pararse
de repente en las sementeras,
se volvía no sé qué Arcángel
reverberando de su fuego.

Más confusión, absurdo y grito
verla dormida en donde fuera.
El largo fuego liso y quieto
no era retama ni era centella.

THE SHAGGY WOMAN

We saw her grow up wild,
cloaked, covered,
and dressed in her tresses.
And we love her and follow her
05   and count her beloved.

Her disordered locks
would fly all around
the shaggy-haired girl
like the grass of the meadows.

10   Pain of startled eyes,
pain of open mouth and laughter.
At the hair of smoke puffs,
of high masts and banners.
She had no face, voice, or age,
15   just pulses of wild flame,
burning tall or trailing
like a feverish bramble.

She'd spy us in an embrace
and our hearts would stop
20   from surprise. The stronger
the wind crossing the plain,
the stronger grew the temptation
to smother or bank that bonfire.

And if she happened to stand up
25   suddenly in the seedbeds,
she turned into some Archangel
reverberating in its flames.

More mayhem, absurd and a scream
to see her asleep there wherever.
30   The long fire, smooth and calm,
wasn't brush nor was it spark.

¿Qué sería ese río ardiendo
y bajo el fuego, qué hacía ella?

Detrás de su totoral
o carrizal, viva y burlesca,
existía sin mirarnos
como quien burla y quien husmea
sabiendo todo de nosotros,
pero sin darnos respuesta . . .

Mata de pastos nunca vista,
cómo la hacía sorda y ciega.
No recordamos, no le vimos
frente, ni espaldas, ni hombreras,
ni vestidos estrenados,
sólo las manos desesperadas
que ahuyentaban sus cabellos
partiéndose como mimbrera.
Una sola cosa de viva
y la misma cosa de muerta.

Galanes la cortejaban
por acercársele y tenerla
un momento separando
mano terca y llama en greñas,
y se dejaba sin dejarse,
verídica y embustera.

Al comer no se la veía
ni al tejer sus lanas sueltas.
Sus cóleras y sus gozos
se le quedaban tras esas rejas.
Era un cerrado capullo denso,
almendra apenas entreabierta.

Se quemaron unos trigales
en donde hacía la siesta;
y a los pinos chamuscaba
con sólo pasarles cerca.

What could that burning river be
and what did she do, beneath the fire?

Bright and mocking behind
35   her canebrake or reedfield,
she lived without looking at us
as one who scoffs and sniffs
knowing everything about us,
but giving us no response . . .

40   Mop of grasses never seen,
how it made her deaf and blind.
We don't recall, we didn't see
a forehead, back, or shoulders,
nor any brand-new dresses,
45   only the desperate hands
that beat back her hair
parting like willow fronds.
One single thing in life
and the same thing in death.

50   Gallants paid court to her
to get close and have her,
one moment separating
stubborn hand and tangled flame,
and she'd let them without letting them,
55   guileless deceiver.

She was never seen to eat
nor to plait her loose fleeces.
Her rages and her joys
remained behind those bars.
60   She was a thick closed cocoon,
an almond scarcely opened.

A few wheatfields burned
where she took her siesta;
and she'd scorch the pines
65   by just passing near them.

Se le quemaron día a día
carne, huesos, y linfas frescas,
todo caía a sus pies,
pero no su cabellera.

Quisieron ponerla abajo,
apagarla con la tierra.
En una caja de cristales
pusimos su rojo cometa.

Esas dulces quemaduras
que nos pintan como a cebras.
La calentura del estío,
lo dorado de nuestros ojos
o lo rojo de nuestra lengua.

Son los aniversarios
de los velorios y las fiestas,
de la niña entera y ardiente
que sigue ardiendo bajo la tierra.

Cuando ya nos acostemos
a su izquierda o a su diestra,
tal vez será arder siempre
brillar como red abierta,
y por ella no tener frío
aunque se muera nuestra planeta.

Flesh, bones, and fresh fluids
burned away day by day,
it all fell at her feet,
but not her mane of hair.

70 They tried to put her out,
extinguish her with earth.
In a casket of glass
we put her red comet.

Those sweet burn-scars
75 that paint us like zebras.
The fever of summer,
the gilding of our eyes
or the red of our tongue.

They are the remembrances
80 of the wakes and the parties,
of the girl pure and fiery
who keeps burning underground.

When we at last lie down
on her left side or her right,
85 it may be to burn always,
to glow like an open grate,
and be kept by her from cold
even though our planet dies.

LA CONTADORA

Cuando camino se levantan
todas las cosas de la Tierra,
y se paran y cuchichean
y es su historia lo que cuentan.

Y las gentes que caminan,
en la ruta me la dejan
y la recojo de caída
en capullos que son de huellas.

Historias corren mi cuerpo
o en mi regazo ronronean.
Zumban, hierven y abejean.
Sin llamada se me vienen
y contadas tampoco me dejan.

Las que bajan por los árboles
se trenzan y se destrenzan,
y me tejen y me envuelven
hasta que el mar las ahuyenta.
Pero el mar que cuenta siempre
y más rendida, más me deja . . .

Los que están mascando bosque
y los que rompen la piedra,
al dormirse quieren historias.

Mujeres que buscan hijos
perdidos que no regresan
y las que se creen vivas
y no saben que están muertas,
cada noche piden historias
y yo me rindo cuenta que cuenta.

THE STORYTELLER

When I walk all the things
of the earth awaken,
and they rise up and whisper
and it's their stories that they tell.

05   And the peoples who wander
leave them for me on the road
and I gather them where they've fallen
in cocoons made of footprints.

Stories run through my body
10   or purr in my lap.
They buzz, boil, and bee-drone.
They come to me uncalled
and don't leave me once told.

Those that come down from the trees
15   braid and unbraid themselves,
and weave me and wrap me
until the sea drives them away.
But the sea speaks endlessly
and the more I tire, the more it tells me . . .

20   People who are chewing the forest
and those who break stone
want stories at bedtime.

Women looking for lost
children who don't return
25   and women who think they're alive
and don't know that they're dead,
ask for stories every night
and I spend myself telling and telling.

A medio camino quedo
entre ríos que no me sueltan,
y el corro se va cerrando
y me atrapan en la rueda.

Al pulgar llegan las de animales
al índice las de mis muertos.
Las de niños, de ser tantas,
en las palmas me hormiguean.

Los marineros alocados
que las piden, ya no navegan,
y las que cuentan se las digo
delante de la mar abierta.

Tuve una que iba en vuelo
de albatroses y tijeretas.
Se oía el viento, se lamía
la sal del mar contenta.
La olvidé de tierra adentro
como el pez que no alimentan.

¿En dónde estará una historia
que volando en gaviota ebria
cayó a mis faldas un día
y de tan blanca me dejó ciega?

Otra mujer cuenta lejos
historia que salva y libera,
tal vez la tiene, tal vez la trae
hasta mi puerta antes que muera.

Cuando tomaba así mis brazos
el que yo tuve, todas ellas
en regato de sangre corrían
mis brazos una noche entera.
Ahora yo, vuelta al Oriente,
se las voy dando por que recuerde.

I stop in the middle of the road
30   between rivers that won't let me go,
and the chorus begins closing in
and they trap me in the ring.

At my thumb come those of the animals,
at my forefinger those of my dead.
35   Those of children, being so many,
swarm like ants on my palms.

The crackpot mariners
who ask for them sail no more,
and those they tell I tell them
40   in front of the open sea.

I had one that went like the flight
of albatrosses and scissortails.
You could hear the wind in it,
it lapped sea-salt contentedly.
45   I forgot it when I was inland
like a fish nobody feeds.

Where could the story be,
flying like a drunken gull,
that fell at my skirts one day
50   and left me blind from such whiteness?

Another faraway woman tells
a story that saves and frees,
maybe she has it, maybe she'll bring it
to my door before she dies.

55   When the one I had took my arms
like this, they all would run
like rivulets of blood
through my arms all night long.
Now, facing East, I'm giving them
60   to that one as a reminder.

Los viejos las quieren mentidas,
los niños las piden ciertas.
Todos quieren oír la historia mía
que en mi lengua viva está muerta.
Busco alguna que la recuerde,
hoja por hoja, hebra por hebra.
Le presto mi aliento, le doy mi marcha
por si al oírla me la despierta.

The old ones want them falsified,
the children beg that they be true.
They all want to hear my own story
which on my living tongue is dead.
65   I search for someone who remembers it,
page for page, thread for thread.
I'll lend them my breath, give them my beat
to see if hearing it wakes it in me.

ELECTRA EN LA NIEBLA

En la niebla marina voy perdida,
yo, Electra, tanteando mis vestidos
y el rostro que en horas fui mudada.
Ahora sólo soy la que ha matado.
Será tal vez a causa de la niebla
que así me nombro por reconocerme.

Quise ver muerto al que mató y lo he visto
o no fue él lo que vi, que fue la Muerte.
Ya no me importa lo que me importaba.
Ya ella no respira el mar Egeo.
Ya está más muda que piedra rodada.
Ya no hace el bien ni el mal. Está sin obras.
Ni me nombra ni me ama ni me odia.
Era mi madre, y yo era su leche,
nada más que su leche vuelta sangre.
Sólo su leche y su perfil, marchando o dormida.
Camino libre sin oír su grito,
que me devuelve y sin oír sus voces,
pero ella no camina, está tendida.
Y la vuelan en vano sus palabras,
sus ademanes, su nombre y su risa,
mientras que yo y Orestes caminamos
tierra de Hélade Ática, suya y de nosotros.
Y cuando Orestes sestee a mi costado
la mejilla sumida, el ojo oscuro,
veré que, como en mí, corren su cuerpo
las manos de ella que lo enmallataron
y que la nombra con sus cuatro sílabas
que no se rompen y no se deshacen.
Porque se lo dijimos en el alba
y en el anochecer y el duro nombre
vive sin ella por más que está muerta.
Y a cada vez que los dos nos miremos,
caerá su nombre como cae el fruto
resbalando en guiones de silencio.

ELECTRA IN THE MIST

In the ocean mist I wander lost,
I, Electra, fingering my garments
and my face, for in hours I was changed.
Now I am merely one who has killed.
05   It could be, perhaps, because of the mist
that I take this name, to know who I am.

I wanted to see the killer dead and I've seen it—
or it wasn't him I saw, but Death.
Now what mattered to me no longer matters.
10   Now she doesn't breathe the Aegean Sea.
Now she's more dumb than a tumbled stone.
Now she does no good or ill. She is without works.
She names me not, loves me not, hates me not.
She was my mother, and I was her milk,
15   nothing more than her milk turned blood.
Only her milk and her profile, moving or asleep.
I walk free without hearing her cry
that turns me back, or hearing her plaints;
but she doesn't walk, she lies stretched out.
20   And her words fly from her in vain,
her gestures, her name and her laugh,
while I and Orestes wander the land
of Attic Hellas, hers and ours.
And when Orestes nods at my side
25   his cheek sunken, his eye dark,
I'll see that on his body, as on mine,
run the hands of her who ensnared it
and that he names her with her four syllables
that never unravel and never wear out.
30   Because we said it to her in the dawn
and in the growing dark, and the hard name
lives without her although she's dead.
And every time we look at each other,
her name will fall as fruit falls
35   slipping out like silent banners.

Sólo a Ifigenia y al amante amaba
por angostura de su pecho frío.
A mí y a Orestes nos dejó sin besos,
sin tejer nuestros dedos con los suyos.
Orestes, no te sé rumbo y camino.
Si esta noche estuvieras a mi lado,
oiría yo tu alma, tú la mía.

Esta niebla salada borra todo
lo que habla y endulza al pasajero:
rutas, puentes, pueblos, árboles.
No hay semblante que mire y reconozca
no más la niebla de mano insistente
que el rostro nos recorre y los costados.

A dónde vamos yendo, los huidos,
si el largo nombre recorre la boca
o cae y se retarda sobre el pecho
como el hálito de ella, y sus facciones,
que vuelan disueltas, acaso buscándome.

El habla niña nos vuelve y resbala
por nuestros cuerpos, Orestes, mi hermano,
y los juegos pueriles, y tu acento.

Husmea mi camino y ven Orestes.
Está la noche acribillada de ella,
abierta de ella, y viviente de ella.
Parece que no tiene palabra
ni otro viajero, ni otro santo y seña.
Pero en llegando el día ha de dejarnos.
¿Por qué no duerme al lado del Egisto.
Será que pende siempre de su seno
la leche que nos dio será eso eterno
y será que esta sal que trae el viento
no es del aire marino, es de su leche?

She loved only her lover and Iphigenia
in the narrowness of her cold breast.
Orestes and me she left without kisses,
without weaving our fingers in hers.
40   Orestes, I don't know your course or your road.
If tonight you were here at my side,
I would hear your soul, and you mine.

This salt mist blots out everything
that comforts and speaks to the traveler:
45   roads, bridges, towns, trees.
There's no face I might see and know,
only the mist whose insistent hand
runs over our faces and flanks.

Where are we going to go, we fugitives,
50   if the long name hangs in our mouths
or falls and lingers over our breasts
as her breath does, and her features
that drift scattered, perhaps looking for me?

Childish speech returns to us and slips
55   through our bodies, Orestes my brother,
and our childhood games, and your accent.

Scent my trail and come, Orestes.
The night itself is riddled with her,
wide with her, and alive with her.
60   It seems that it has no word
or other traveler, no other secret sign.
But when day comes, she must leave us.
Why doesn't she sleep beside Aegisthus?
Could it be that the milk she gave us
65   still drips from her breast, and always will,
and that this salt the wind bears
comes not from the sea air, but from her milk?

Apresúrate, Orestes, ya que seremos
dos siempre, dos, como manos cogidas
o los pies corredores de la tórtola huida.
No dejes que yo marche en esta noche
rumbo al desierto y tanteando en la niebla.

Yo no quiero saber, pero quisiera
saberlo todo de tu boca misma,
cómo cayó, qué dijo dando el grito
y si te dio maldición o te bendijo.
Espérame en el cruce del camino
en donde hay piedras lajas y unas matas
de menta y de romero, que confortan.

Porque ella—tú la oyes—ella llama,
y siempre va a llamar, y es preferible
morir los dos sin que nadie nos vea
de puñal, Orestes, y morir de propia muerte.
—El dios que te movió nos dé esta gracia.
—Y las tres gracias que a mí me movieron.
—Están como medidos los alientos.
—Donde los dos se rompan pararemos.
La niebla tiene pliegues de sudario
dulce en el palpo, en la boca salobre
y volverás a ir al canto mío.
Siempre viviste lo que yo vivía
por otro atajo irás y al lado mío.
Tal vez la niebla es tu aliento y mis pasos
los tuyos son por desnudos y heridos.
Pero por qué tan callado caminas
y vas a mi costado sin palabras,
el paso enfermo y el perfil humoso,
si por ser uno lo mismo quisimos
y cumplimos lo mismo y nos llamamos
Electra-Oreste, yo, tú, Oreste-Electra?
O yo soy niebla que corre sin verse
o tú niebla que corre sin saberse.
—Pare yo por que puedas detenerte
o yo me tumbe, para detenerte con mi cuerpo tu carrera;

Make haste, Orestes, now that we'll be
two forever; two, like clasped hands
70   or the running feet of a flushed dove.
Don't leave me to follow this night course
to the desert, feeling my way in the mist.

I don't want to know, but I would like
to know it all from your own mouth,
75   how she fell, what she said when she screamed
and whether she cursed or blessed you.
Wait for me at the crossroads
where there are flat stones and some clumps
of mint and rosemary to comfort us.

80   Because she—you hear her—she's calling,
and is always going to call, and it's better
both of us die by the dagger without anyone
seeing us, Orestes, and die a fit death.
  —May the god that moved you give us this grace.
85   —And the three graces that moved me.
  —It's as if our breaths are numbered.
  —Where the two are sundered we'll stop.
The mist is gathered like a shroud,
soft on the tongue and brackish in the mouth,
90   and you'll come back to walk to my song.
You always lived what I was living;
you'll take a shortcut and go by my side.
Perhaps the mist is your breath and my paces
are yours, for they're bare and wounded.
95   But why do you walk so quietly
and go beside me without a word,
your step unsteady and your profile hazy,
if being one we desired the same thing
and did the same deed and called ourselves
100   Electra-Orestes, I; you, Orestes-Electra?
Either I'm mist that flows without seeing
or you're mist that flows without knowing.
  —Whether I halt so you might stay a while
or take a fall, to stay your course with my body,

tal vez todo fue sueño de nosotros
adentro de la niebla amoratada
befa de la niebla que vuela sin sentido.
Pero marchar me rinde y necesito
romper la niebla o que me rompa ella.
Si alma los dos tuvimos, que nuestra alma
—siga marchando y que nos abandone.
—Ella es quien va pasando y no la niebla.
Era una sola en un solo palacio
y ahora es niebla-albatrós, niebla-camino,
niebla-mar, niebla-aldea, niebla-barco.
Y aunque mató y fue muerta ella camina
más ágil y ligera que en su cuerpo
y así es que nos rendimos sin rendirla.
Orestes, hermano, te has dormido
caminando o de nada te acuerdas
que no respondes.

105 perhaps it was all a dream of ours
     within the bruise-colored mist,
     a taunt of the mist that drifts senselessly.
     But walking exhausts me and I need
     to breach the mist or it will break me.
110 If ever we two had a soul, let our soul
     —keep on walking and leave us behind.
     —It's she who is passing and not the mist.
     She was a woman alone in one lone palace
     and now she's a mist-albatross, a mist-road,
115 a mist-sea, a mist-village, a mist-ship.
     And though she killed and was dead, she walks
     more agile and lighter than in her body
     and so we spend ourselves without tiring her.
     Orestes, brother, you've fallen asleep
120 walking or else you remember nothing
     for you don't answer.

MADRE BISOJA

Ésta que era nuestra Madre,
la Tierra sombría y sacra
y era tan vieja y tan niña
que al verla se desvariaba.

Era la higuera de leche
y era la Osa encrespada
y era más, de ser la Loca
que da su flanco por dádiva.

Arqueaba el cielo su brazo
dándola por ahijada
y ella lo miraba absorta
de recibirlo en cascada.

Y lo mismo la llamaban
la Verdeante que la Parda,
o la Niña Dedos-Cortos,
o la Mujer Manos-Anchas.

Por el ajetrear de día
y hacer de noche jornada,
casa techada no quiso,
de intemperie enamorada.

A todas las criaturas
soportó en rodillas anchas
y rebosando, ninguna
se le cayó de la falda.

Y conturbaba su encuentro
por ser bisoja y doblada,
que un ojo suyo era negro
y el otro color genciana.

CROSS-EYED MOTHER

This was once our Mother,
the shady and sacred Earth
and she was so old and so childish
whoever saw her would wonder.

05   She was the milky fig tree
and she was the bristling She-Bear
and more, being the Mad One
who gives her flank in bounty.

The sky would arch his arm
10   taking her under his care
and she would watch entranced
to receive him in a shower.

And they'd as easily call her
the Green One as the Brown,
15   or the Girl with Short Fingers,
or the Broad-Handed Woman.

What with daytime's bustle
and making a progress of night,
she didn't want a roofed house,
20   loving the open sky.

She held all the creatures
in her capacious lap
and, overflowing, not one
ever fell from her skirt.

25   And to meet her was disturbing
for she was cross-eyed and bent,
since one of her eyes was black
and the other the color of gentian.

A causa del ojo azul
el día se adelantaba
y por el ojo sombrío
la noche abría sus arcas.

En abriendo el ojo azul
se le iban a la zaga
acónitos y verbenas
siguiéndola que volaban.

Y tanto el azul crecía
que se volvía mañana
y todo el azul del mundo
sólo ella lo pastoreaba.

Cuando el ojo azul dormía
el negro se despertaba
y desde entonces él solo
regía en cuerpos y almas.

Entonces detrás de Gea
se iban veras y fantasmas;
y abiertas las bocaminas
sus engendros bostezaban.

Iban al trote los topos
ladeando las musarañas
y de marcha y procesión
la gran noche rebosaba.

Y la bisoja iba abriendo
la noche como a tajadas,
y la procesión seguía
por sus quiebros y sus abras.

Cuando al alba de regreso
la Madre era interrogada,
Gea, jugando a dos mundos,
ni levantaba la cara.

On account of the blue eye
30   the day would hurry forward
and for the shadowed eye
night opened its coffers.

On opening, the blue eye
would leave a scattered trail
35   of aconites and verbenas
following her in flight.

And the blue grew so large
that it turned into morning
and she alone would shepherd
40   all the blue in the world.

When the blue eye slept
the black one would awaken
and in bodies and souls
from then on ruled alone.

45   Then in back of Gaea
trailed hard facts and phantoms;
and, the mineshafts opening,
her low spawn yawned out.

The moles went at a trot
50   pushing the shrews aside
and with marching and procession
the great night overflowed.

And the cross-eyed one went opening
the night as if in slices,
55   and the procession followed
through her fissures and her gorges.

When the Mother was questioned
at the return of day,
Gaea, playing at two worlds,
60   wouldn't even lift her face.

Y cuando se le reían
ella sonriendo callaba
y a causa de su silencio
sus hijos la fabulaban.

Dicen que no envejeció
ni en el rostro ni en la marcha,
aunque envejecieron todos
los que ella amamantara.

Que le hicieron una tumba
para la hora llegada
y ella reía, reía,
de ver cómo la cavaban.

Así era cuando nací
y es a mi tarde sesgada
y de sabido lo cuento
como quien dice charada.

And when they laughed at her
she smiled and held her peace
and on account of her silence
her children made up tales.

65   They say she didn't age
in her face or in her step,
though everyone grew old
that she had ever suckled.

They made her a tomb
70   for the hour that had come
and she laughed and laughed
to see how they would dig it.

So it was when I was born
and is, in the twilight of my day
75   and I tell, from what is known,
what you might call a charade.

LA QUE AGUARDA

Antes del umbral y antes de la ruta,
aguardo, aguardo al que camina recto
y avanza recto mejor que agua y fuego.

Viene a causa de mí, viene por mí,
no por albergue ni por pan y vino,
a causa de que yo soy su alimento
y soy el vaso que él alza y apura.

Del bosque que lo envuelve en leño y trinos,
y sombras temblorosas que lo trepan,
se arranca, y viene, y llega sin soslayo,
porque lo trae mi rasgado grito.

Va pasando las torres que lo atajan
con sus filos de témpanos agudos
y llega, sin salmueras, de dos mares,
indemne como en forro y vaina de honda.

¡Y ahora ya la mano que lo alcanza
afirma su cintura en la carrera!

Y saben, sí, saben mi cuerpo y mi alma
que viene caminando por la raya
amoratada de mi propio grito,
sin enredarse en el fresno glorioso
ni relajarse en las densas arenas.

¡Cómo no ha de llegar si me lo traen
los elementos a los que fui dada!
El agua me lo alumbra en los hondones,
me lo apresura el fuego del poniente
y el viento loco lo aguija y apura.

Vilano o pizca ebria parecía;
apenas era y ya no voltijea,
nonadas de la niebla lo sorbían

SHE WHO WAITS

Before the threshold and before the path,
    * I wait and wait for one who walks straight
and advances truer than water or fire.

He comes because of me, he comes for me,
05   not for shelter, nor for bread and wine,
but because of the fact that I'm his food
and I'm the cup that he lifts and drains.

From the forest that wraps him in timber and trills,
and trembling shadows that climb him,
10   he sets out, and comes, and arrives undeflected
because my rending shout brings him.

He goes past the towers that cut him off
with their sharp-edged icebergs
and arrives, brineless, from two seas,
15   unharmed as in a deep plush sheath.

And already the hand that reaches to him
steadies his waist on the way!

And they know, yes my body and soul know
that he comes walking the livid
20   ribbon of my own shout, without
entangling himself in the glorious ash-tree
or resting on the hard-packed sands.

How could he not arrive, if the elements
I'm pledged to bring him to me!
25   The water lights him for me in the depths,
the fire of the sunset hurries him to me
and the mad wind pricks and spurs him.

He seemed a thistledown or drunken splinter;
was scarcely there, but he no longer whirls,
30   wisps of mist swallowed him up

desbaratando su juego de mástiles
y sus saltos de ciervo despeñado.
Del bosque que lo envuelve en sus rumores
se suelta y ya se viene sin soslayo.
Viene más puro que disco lanzado;
más recto vuela que albatros sediento
porque lo trae mi rasgado grito,
y el grito mío no se le relaja:
ciego y exacto como el alma llega.
Abre ya, parte, el matorral intruso
y todavía mi voz enlazada
con sus cabellos el paso le aviva.
Y al acercarse ya suelta su espalda;
libre lo deja y se apaga en su rostro.
Pero mi grito sólo sube recto,
su mano ya cae a mi puerta.

tearing apart his set of masts
and his headlong deer-leaps.
He breaks free of the forest that wraps him
in rumors and now he comes undeflected.
35   He comes more pure than a hurled discus;
he flies straighter than a thirsty albatross
because my rending shout brings him,
and my shout doesn't loosen its grip:
he arrives blind and exact as the soul.
40   The choking thicket parts, it opens now
and even so my voice entwined
in his hair quickens his step.
And now as he nears it releases his back;
it lets him go and fades from his face.
45   But my shout alone rises upright,
his hand already falls at my door.

DOS TRASCORDADOS

Anduvimos trocados por la tierra,
él por las costas, yo por las llanuras,
él dispersado entre materias ciegas,
yo desvariando nombre que era el suyo,
zarandeados del agua y del fuego
y husmeados de la loba y la [. . .]
y sin comer y beber alimentos,
sólo mordiendo por granada el pecho.

Nos cruzamos en noche de ventisca;
en las mismas posadas estuvimos,
ciegos dormidos y ciegos despiertos.
De la vigilia ya desconfiamos;
si es que estamos soñando, que soñemos;
hasta que nos convenza nuestro sueño.

Está el pasado cayendo en pedazos
como el mendigo de las ropas bufas . . .
no lloramos viéndonos desnudos,
ni tiritamos de tanto despojo;
si tanto falta es que nada tuvimos.

Todos partieron y estamos quedados
sobre una ruta que sigue y nos deja.
Y no lloramos cuando desprendimos
sus pobres manos de su ronda muerta.
Si todo ha sido sueño y desvaríos
que me madure en el sueño la muerte.

TWO FORGOTTEN ONES

We walked changed through the land,
he by the coasts, I on the plains,
he scattered through blind matter,
I raving the name that was his—
05   winnowed from the water and the fire,
and stalked by the she-wolf and the [. . .]
and without drinking or eating food,
gnawing only the pomegranate in my breast.

We crossed paths on the night of a blizzard;
10   we stayed in the same lodgings,
blind in sleep and blind awake.
Already we mistrust wakefulness;
if we are dreaming, then let us dream,
until our dream convinces us.

15   The past is falling to pieces
like the beggar with his clown-clothes . . .
we don't cry seeing ourselves naked,
nor do we shiver at so much waste;
if so much is missing, it's that we had nothing.

20   Everyone left and we have remained
on a path that goes on without us.
And we didn't cry when we loosened
his poor hands from his dance of death
If it's all been dream and delirium
25   may death ripen me in my dream.

LA TROCADA

Así no fue como me amaron
y camino como en la infancia
y ando ahora desatentada.
Serían aquellos metales
donde el amor tuvo peana.
Serían los duros líquenes,
el descampado, la venteada,
o los pardos alimentos
—piñon, y cardo y avellana—
si me amaban como se odia
y al Amor mismo avergonzaban.

El montañés miró mi rostro
como la ruta con celada.
Para su amor fui la lobezna
por peñascales rastreada.
A los engendros de la noche
se fiaban más que a mi alma,
veía el duende de la niebla,
los espejos de la avalancha,
y nunca oyó mi canto ardiendo
sobre su puerta con escarcha . . .

En el país de la gaviota
del aire suyo voy llevada
y le pregunto al que me lleva
por qué, en bajando, fui trocada,
y me creen sobre las dunas
y en salinas yo he sido salva.

Y camino como la niña,
aprendiendo tierra mudada,
clara patria color de leche,
lento olivar, lindas aguadas,

THE CHANGED WOMAN

This was not how they loved me
and I walk as in childhood
and wander now unheeding.
Those metals would be
05   where love set his pedestal.
So would the tough lichens,
the exposed, the windblown,
or the wild brown food
—pine-nut, and thistle and filbert—
10   if they loved me as people hate
and they'd put Love himself to shame.

The mountain-dweller saw my face
as a path set with an ambush.
For his love I was the young wolf
15   tracked through the rocky peaks.
They trusted the spawn
of night more than my soul;
the snow demon was seeing
the mirrors of the avalanche,
20   and never heard my song burning
over his frost-rimmed door . . .

In the land of the seagull
I'm being carried on his wind
and I ask the one who bears me
25   why, on landing, I was changed,
and they believe me on the dunes
and in the salt pools I've been saved.

And I wander like a girl
learning a land transformed,
30   bright homeland the color of milk,
slow olive grove, lovely waters;

oyendo pido cantos no sabidos,
teniendo hermanas iguanas
y ¡con extrañeza, con asombro,
y azoro de resucitada!

listening I ask for unknown songs,
possessing iguana sisters
and with the strangeness, the wonder,
35   and alarm of the resurrected!

UNCOLLECTED

CLITEMNESTRA

Saben las bestezuelas por el aire
y las diez fuentes por el gran grito
que Agamenón echó sobre la hoguera
como pino-ciprés o vil mastuerzo
a la cordera que durmió en mis brazos,
que mi leche mamó como el cervato
y, por mi leche, blanca fue y ligera.

Vino el rasgado grito de la plebe
falto de brisas hacia estas mil puertas,
cuando su espalda de color de los mirtos
cayó a la llama y la tomó la llama.
La plebe aúlla contra el cielo
como ebria, azuzada por el fuego,
el nombre de su Rey y no el de mi cordera,
danza y eructa gritos de victoria,
hormiguea sorda de tambores,
eructa, baila, berreando a sus dioses,
y la Ifigenia cae, cae, cae,
mientras yo, enmurallada en torno de la hoguera,
me rasguño las puertas atoradas del palacio.

Pero yo veo, veo, veo, veo,
a despecho de leguas y humaredas,
veo brincar las llamas de la hoguera
que cabritos la trepan o la bajan
o en lienzos retorcidos de humo y fuego
que esconden y me dan a la Cordera
y son sus brazos de gaviota al vuelo,
son sus cabellos de suspiro ardiente
y veo hombros y el cuello de su gracia.
Y el Oso helado que me llevó al lecho
mira al cielo respirando la alta llama.

La plebe en hebra oscura pespuntea
toda la costa, más saciada, con la cara al viento,
babeante, hipando el nombre de sus dioses.

CLYTEMNESTRA

The little creatures know by the air,
and the ten fountains by the great shout,
that Agamemnon cast on the pyre
like cypress-pine or common cress
05 the lamb that slept in my arms,
that suckled my milk like a fawn
and, from my milk, was lithe and white.

The ragged shout of the crowd came
without a breeze to these thousand doors,
10 when her back the color of the myrtles
fell to the flame and the flame took her.
The crowd howls against heaven
as if drunk, whipped up by the fire,
the name of its King and not that of my lamb,
15 it dances and belches victory shouts,
swarms like ants, deafened by drums,
belches, dances, bellowing to its gods,
and she, Iphigenia, falls, falls, falls,
while I, walled in so near the pyre,
20 claw at the bolted palace doors.

But I see, I see, I see, I see,
despite the leagues and clouds of smoke,
I see the flames of the bonfire leap
like kids that clamber up or fall
25 or twisted curtains of smoke and fire
that hide and disclose the Lamb to me
and they are her arms like a gull's in flight,
they are her tresses of burning sighs
and I see shoulders and that graceful neck.
30 And the icy Bear who brought me to bed
gazes at heaven breathing the tall flame.

The crowd embroiders the whole coast
like dark thread, more sated now, face to the wind,
drooling, panting the name of its gods.

Pero yo aquí, detrás de mis cerrojos,
reniego con mi cuerpo y mis potencias
de los dioses que dan y que arrebatan
y del Leopardo Real que engendra y mata.

Las fuentes grávidas más que él entienden.
Sólo me oyen los siervos apiñados.
Puro el grito he de dar que oigan los dioses
si no son sus oídos conchas muertas
y no es su pecho escudo como escarcha
y no son celos polvo del camino.
Mi Ifigenia, partida y devastada,
hecha y deshecha, camina con llama
pura, volteando azules y dorados
y el Rey Leopardo, Agamenón, vuelta la cara
congestionada de soberbia de su loco triunfo
ahora se vuelve al viento y los veleros,
a la vez vencedor y ya vencido.

No te vea yo más, no más yo duerma
tocándote las sienes; no más abras
estas mis puertas y arranques de los brazos
a Electra y Orestes para otra hoguera.
Siento como que va de mí subiendo
otra alma y que me viene como al árbol
otra carne y que las llamas
de Ifigenia me alcanzan y me visten.

Yo no te vuelva a ver, Rey de los hombres,
no subas más las escaleras donde
en triángulo de luz jugaban nuestros hijos.
No me traigas tu gloria de timbales,
ni tus carros crujiendo de trofeos,
ni llegarás a llevarme de rodillas
hacia tus dioses que aúllan cobrando
con el belfo de lobos carne de hijos.

La llama de Ifigenia ya se aleja,
ralea, lame sus propias cenizas.

35 But here, behind my deadbolts, I
    curse with my body and all my powers
    the gods that give and snatch away
    and the Royal Leopard who sires and slays.

    The teeming fountains know more than he.
40 Only the huddled slaves hear me.
    Pure the cry I must give for the gods to hear
    if their ears are not dead shells
    and their breasts not frozen shields
    and their jealousy not mere roadway dust.
45 My Iphigenia, broken and wasted,
    made and unmade, walks with pure
    flame, whirling blues and golds
    and the Leopard King, Agamemnon, face
    swollen with pride at his lunatic triumph,
50 now wheels to the wind and the sailing ships,
    at once victor and vanquished.

    Never more let me see you, never more let me sleep
    touching your temples; never more open
    these my doors and tear from my arms
55 Electra and Orestes for another pyre.
    I feel as if another soul rises from me
    and another flesh comes to me
    as to a tree, and that the flames
    of Iphigenia overtake me and clothe me.

60 May I never see you again, King of men,
    don't ever again climb the stairs where
    our children played in a triangle of light.
    Don't bring me your drummed-up glory,
    or your chariots groaning with trophies,
65 nor will you come to lead me on my knees
    toward your gods that howl, seizing
    with the chops of wolves the flesh of children.

    Iphigenia's flame already recedes,
    wears thin, laps its own ashes.

Yo andaré, sin saberlo, mi camino
hacia el mar cargando en estas manos,
en pez encenizado, la hija mía,
ahora más ligera que sus trenzas,
y de esta brasa todos arderemos,
Agamenón hasta el última día:
tu palacio, tus mirtos, tus palomas,
con un Rey de hombres y una Reina loca.

70   I will walk, unknowing, my road
        toward the sea bearing in these hands,
        like an ashen fish, my daughter,
        lighter now than her tresses,
        and from this coal we all will burn,
75   Agamemnon, unto the last day:
        your palace, your myrtles, your doves,
        with a King of men and a mad Queen.

CASANDRA

A la puerta estoy de mis señores,
blanca de polvo y roja de jornadas,
yo, Casandra de Ilión, a quien amaban
los cerros y los ríos, los seres y las cosas.
Todo me amaba dentro de mi casta,
y sobre el rostro de Ilión todo fue mío,
las islas avisadas y sus semblantes de oro,
todo, menos el turbio día del exilio.
Desnuda estoy de todo lo que tuve:
no amé el amor, he amado al enemigo.
Viajé siguiendo a mi enemigo y dueño,
rehén y amante, suya y extranjera.

Al primer carro de los vencedores,
subí temblando de amor y de destino
en brazos del que amé contra mí misma,
y contra Ilión, la que hizo mis sentidos,
y cuando ya mis pies no la tocaron,
la Patria, enderezada, dio un vagido
como de madre o hembra despojada,
grito de cierva o de viento herido.

En su carro me trajo y en su pecho
y ha cruzado bajíos, colinas, y arenales
y las aldeas arremolinadas,
el vencedor cuyo rostro les da frío.
Y yo no las he visto ni escuchado
de traer en mi bien los ojos fijos.
Cruzó Atenas sin tocar su polvo.
A veces le echó cala de ojos bizcos.
Le veo la señal apresurada,
mas sin el botín de mi cuerpo en sangre tinto.
Saben más mis dioses que los forasteros
y ellos pastorearon mis sentidos.

También, como en Ilión, no valen puertas,
piedras ni bronce para que yo no vea

CASSANDRA

I stand at the door of my lords,
white with dust and red with journeys,
I, Cassandra of Ilion, whom the hills
and rivers loved, the beings and things.
05   All within my caste loved me,
and over the face of Ilion all was mine,
the clear-sighted isles and their features of gold,
all, but for the clouded day of exile.
I am stripped of everything I had:
10   I loved not love, I have loved the enemy.
I traveled following my enemy and master:
hostage and lover, his and yet a stranger.

Into the first chariot of the victors
I mounted, trembling with love and destiny
15   in the arms of him I loved against myself
and against Ilion, she who formed my senses,
and when my feet no longer touched her,
my homeland, rising up, gave a wail
as of a plundered mother or she-creature,
20   the cry of a hind or the wounded wind.

He brought me in his chariot and in his breast
across shoals and hills, sandy beaches
and storm-threshed villages,
the victor whose look strikes them cold.
25   And keeping my eyes fixed on my love,
I neither saw nor heard them.
He crossed Athens without touching its dust.
Sometimes he threw a glance from squinting eyes.
In him I see the hastening sign,
30   but without the prize of my blood-dyed body.
My gods know more than these strangers do
and they shepherded my senses.

Besides, as in Ilion, doors are worthless,
stone or bronze, to prevent my seeing

la hora señalada que camina
hacia mí, sin sesgo ni descanso.
Veo en la niebla y en la nuez de la noche.
Yo soy Casandra, la que, sin pedirlo,
todo lo supo y vino a su destino,
yo, Casandra, llena de miradas,
que ve su propia muerte, sin volverse,
y oye en la noche el día que le sigue.
Desde el abrazo de Apolo, mis ojos
así quedaron, sin cerrar los párpados.
Abre tus pobres puertas poderosas
y mira el rostro de la amante bárbara
tan recta y sin temblor como una flecha.

Ya abre las puertas para recibirnos,
según recibe el cántaro reseco
el chorro de su cidra o de su vino.
Fui para él aquello que no fuiste
con tu cuerpo gastado cual las rutas.
Tal cidra y vino a la vejez fui deseada,
deseada fui como la azul cascada fina
que ataranta los ojos del sediento.
Mira el rostro que tu dueño mira
y en el que se ha tardado por diez años.

A las puertas estoy de hierro y bronce
sabiendo sitio y hora de esa muerte.
Oigo y cuento los pasos presurosos
de la que ya apuró su primer sorbo
y me sale al encuentro, por beber el otro,
Clitemnestra, que me odió antes de verme.
Ya vaciaste su cuerpo que era mío,
y su sangre me anhelaba por las losas.
Ya estás bebiendo el cuerpo que detestas
y yo repaso el que me sabía.
Sangre tiene la voz que me desposa
y tu hálito también y hasta tus gestos.
Todo lo sigo viendo, aquí, a tu puerta,
en tu luz y en tu aire de tu patria,

35 the appointed hour that advances
toward me, without swerve or rest.
I see in the mist and in the kernel of night.
I am Cassandra—she who, without asking,
understood it all and still came to her fate,
40 I, Cassandra, full of visions,
who sees her own death without turning away,
and hears in the night the day that follows.
Since Apollo's embrace, my eyes
stay like this, the lids never closing.
45 Open your poor powerful doors
and behold the face of the barbarian lover
straight and unshaken as an arrow.

Now open the doors to receive us,
the way the dry pitcher receives
50 the gush of its cider or its wine.
I was for him all that you were not
with your body worn out like the roads.
Like cider and aged wine I was desired,
desired like the sheer blue cascade
55 that dazzles the eyes of the thirsty.
Behold the face that your master sees
and in which he has dallied ten years.

I stand at the doors of iron and bronze
knowing the time and place of that death.
60 I hear and count her rapid steps
who has already drained one draft
and comes out to meet me, to drink the other,
Clytemnestra, who hated me before seeing me.
Already you've emptied his body that was mine,
65 while his blood longed for me from the stones.
Already you're drinking the body you hate
and I recall the one who knew me.
The voice that betroths me has blood in it
and your breath too and even your gestures.
70 I keep seeing it all, here, at your door,
in your light, and in your air, your country—

yo rebanada de los míos, yo arrastrada
ya la Hélade en carro de vencidos;
muriéndome le veré, sin demandarlo,
pues sigue y seguirá amándome en el Hades.
Voy, voy, ya sé mi rumbo por la sangre
de Agamenón que en su coral me llama
y sin que se enderece me libera.
No vale, ay, el bronce de la puerta
para que yo no vea a la que viene
por caminos de mirtos a buscarme,
ebria de odio y loca de destino.

Yo soy aquella a quien dejara Apolo,
en prenda de su amor, dos ojos lúcidos.
Sin llanto navegué por mar de llanto,
y bajé de mi carro de cautiva,
sin rehusar, entendiendo y consintiendo.
Esta mujer me rodea en ceñidura,
pero es la sangre de él la que me ciñe
y su hilo de coral es quien lleva
consigo a aquella que es rehén y amada.
Y las puertas se cierran tras aquella
que veinte años lo tuvo sin amarlo,
y a quien yo amé y seguí por mar e islas,
aspirando en la nave las esencias
por retener la Patria en puro aroma.
Ya estamos ya las dos, ricas de púrpura
y de pasión, ganadas y perdidas,
todo entendiendo y todo agradeciendo
al Hado que sabe, une y salva.

Quédate aquí, tardado jarro, recogiendo
el botín de mi Patria y que te vistas
las sedas de mi madre y te resuene
el saqueo de Ilión en la garganta.
Siempre tú irás vestida de dos sangres,
y que no te caliente, que te hiele
la sangre de tu Rey junto a la mía.
Yo te sigo a la señal que me libera.

cut off from my people, dragged the length
of Hellas in a cart full of the vanquished;
dying I'll see him, without asking to,
75   for he keeps and will keep loving me in Hades.
I'm going, going, I know my way by the blood
of Agamemnon whose red chorus calls me
and without rising frees me.
The bronze of the door is worthless, alas,
80   to keep me from seeing her who comes
by the walks of myrtles to search me out
drunk with hatred and crazed by fate.

I am the one to whom Apollo left,
as a pledge of his love, two lucid eyes.
85   Without tears I sailed on a sea of tears,
and stepped down without balking
from my captive's car, understanding and consenting.
This woman envelops me with cinches,
but it's his blood that girds me
90   and his coral thread that bears off with him
the one who is both hostage and beloved.
And the doors close behind that woman
who had him twenty years without loving him,
whom I loved and followed over sea and islands,
95   inhaling essences aboard the ship
to retain the pure aroma of my homeland.
Now the two of us are here at last, rich
in purple and in passion, won and lost,
understanding all and grateful for all
100   to the Fate that knows, unites, and saves.

Stay here, belated vessel, gathering up
the bounty of my homeland, and may you wear
the silks of my mother and may the sack
of Ilion resound in your throat.
105   You will always go dressed in two bloods,
and may the blood of your King joined
with mine never warm you, but freeze you.
I follow you at the sign that sets me free.

Ya me tumban tus sanguinarios siervos,
ya me levantan en faisán cazado,
pero el otro faisán de tu deseo,
después de su muerte y de tu hartazgo,
te dejará el despojo de sus siervos,
y antes del alba, yo habré recuperado
al Rey de Hombres en el eterno vuelo.
Agamenón, ya voy, ya voy, de vuelo.

Now your bloodthirsty slaves throw me down,
110   now they hoist me like a hunted pheasant,
but the other pheasant of your desire,
after his death and your satisfaction,
will leave you as spoils for his servants,
and before the dawn, I'll have found again
115   the King of Men on the eternal flight.
Agamemnon, I'm coming, I come flying.

TEXTS AND SOURCES

I revise more than people would believe, revisiting some poems that even in their published versions still feel unpolished to me. I left a labyrinth of hills behind me, and something of that untangleable knot survives in whatever I create, be it poems or prose.[1]

Spanish texts for the sixteen *Locas mujeres* poems published during Mistral's lifetime in *Lagar* largely follow the 1968 fourth edition of the *Poesías completas,* published originally in Madrid by Aguilar in 1958 as part of its Biblioteca Premios Nobel. Mistral collaborated with the editor, Margaret Bates, early in the preparation of this collection, changing the order of poems from that in *Lagar* and establishing "definitive" versions of the texts, authorized by Mistral's companion and literary executor Doris Dana. I have silently restored missing line-end punctuation in two places, following the 1954 first edition of *Lagar.*

In the Translator's Note to her 1961 bilingual *Selected Poems of Gabriela Mistral,* Dana, who had worked with Mistral on her papers, announced: "A second posthumous book of poems, *Lagar II,* along with several volumes of Gabriela's prose works which I have compiled and edited, will be published soon by Aguilar in Madrid." That publication never came to pass. The texts of the poems destined for the project exist in a typescript entitled *Lagar II,* with numerous manuscript corrections and annotations in several hands including Mis-

---

1 "Corrijo bastante más de lo que la gente puede creer, leyendo unos versos que aún así me quedan bárbaros. Salí de un laberinto de cerros y algo de ese nudo sin desatadura posible, queda en lo que hago, sea verso o sea prosa." Gabriela Mistral, "Como escribo (How I Write)" in *Gabriela Mistral: Selected Prose and Prose-Poems,* edited and translated by Stephen Tapscott (Austin: University of Texas Press, 2002), 207.

tral's. Microfilms of this typescript and of many holograph working papers relating to the *Locas mujeres* poems are available to scholars at the Library of Congress Manuscript Division in Washington, D.C. References to the typescript in my notes are to series I, reel 1 of the Gabriela Mistral Papers (microfilm).

In 1991, Pedro Pablo Zegers, working from a copy of the microfilm acquired by the Chilean government, published an edition of *Lagar II*. Zegers, with the collaboration of Ana María Cuneo and others, identified manuscript corrections and notations by Mistral and Dana and worked to follow their intent. The Zegers edition notes textual variants in the annotated typescript and silently adjusts punctuation and, occasionally, stanza division. References to Zegers in my notes are to this edition.

Gastón von dem Bussche, who worked with Dana to organize and classify Mistral's papers for microfilming, asserted that the poems of *Lagar II* formed an integral part, with *Lagar,* of a single work that had been divided on the advice of its publishers in order to reduce its length (see his introduction to *Lagar II*). Griñor Rojo considered it more likely that the poems represented later compositions pertaining to the same thematic group.[2] Luis Vargas Saavedra advanced the controversial claim that *Lagar II,* despite the typescript's advanced state of ordering and holograph corrections, represented a group of "rejects" by the poet.[3] Given that during her lifetime Mistral shifted poems from one published collection to another as they were reprinted, and given her carelessness about collecting her work and her habit of obsessive revision, it may never be possible to determine what relationship she intended the *Lagar II* poems to have to the published version of *Lagar*. The *Lagar II* text has been included in several anthologies and the poems are widely studied, so the question may retain only scholarly interest.

At least three of the *Locas mujeres* poems in *Lagar II* received noteworthy individual publication prior to Zegers's volume. "La trocada" first appeared in the Sunday, February 15, 1942, edition of the Bue-

2 Griñor Rojo, *Dirán que está en la gloria—: Mistral* (Santiago: Fondo de Cultura Económica, 1997), 391–95.

3 Luis Vargas Saavedra, "Lagar II de Gabriela Mistral," in *Gabriela Mistral: Nuevas visiones, Estudios Filológicos* Supplement 13 (Valdivia: Universidad Austral de Chile, 1989), 114.

nos Aires daily *La Nación.* Appended to this version is the dateline "Petrópolis, febrero de 1942." References to *La Nación* in my notes are to this version.

A version of "La contadora" was included by the Uruguayan physician and poet Esther de Cáceres in her introduction to the Aguilar *Poesías completas.* About her source for the poem she says, "Unpublished poems by Gabriela Mistral have come to hand, about which Doris Dana had spoken to me, and which she has now given me to read, with a generosity for which I thank her from my soul."[4] References to Cáceres in my notes are to this publication.

"Electra en la niebla" appeared in issue 27 (July-September 1963) of *La Palabra y el Hombre,* a review published by the Universidad Veracruzana, with the following headnote: "Our review has the honor of publishing these two unpublished poems through the courtesy of the writer Doris Dana, Gabriela Mistral's executor. These poems pertain to the second *Lagar* which will shortly be published by Editorial Losada of Argentina."[5] References to *La Palabra* in my notes are to this version.

"Electra en la niebla" appeared again in the first issue (July 1966) of the important Paris-based review *Mundo Nuevo,* edited by Uruguayan exile Emir Rodríguez Monegal. References to *Mundo Nuevo* in my notes are to this version. The poem was also included in a special 1967 combined edition, honoring Mistral, of the Chilean journal *Orfeo.* This publication omits the fourth line and otherwise differs in minor ways from the first two; I have not noted the variants.

In his 1983 compilation *Reino,* von dem Bussche included a version of "Electra" informed by his work on the Mistral papers (as well as reprinting Cáceres's text of "La contadora"). This version seems to have been superseded by that in Zegers's volume, to which von dem Bussche contributed a prologue; I have not drawn from it.

Mistral, as noted above, was notorious for continuing to revise poems that had already been published, sometimes through several

---

4 "Han llegado a mis manos poemas inéditos de Gabriela Mistral, de los que Doris Dana me había hablado, y que ahora me ha dado a leer, con una generosidad que le agradezco desde lo mejor de mi alma."
5 "Nuestra revista tiene el honor de publicar estos dos poemas inéditos, por cortesía de la escritora Doris Dana, albacea de Gabriela Mistral. Estos poemas pertenecen al segundo LAGAR que será próximamente publicado por la Editorial Losada de Argentina."

printed versions. And as Zegers cautions in his introduction to *Lagar II*, the poems of the corrected typescript retain to varying degrees the character of "works in progress." Thus no single source text claims definitive status for the eight *Locas mujeres* poems in this group. In preparing my Spanish texts, several contending principles influenced my choices.

First, that Mistral's last known decisions should be respected. In the *Lagar II* group, this principle privileged the corrected typescript, on which the poet and Doris Dana were working in the final years of her life, over earlier publications.

In the cases of "La contadora" and "Electra en la niebla," the versions published within a few years after the poet's death, while Dana's memory of Mistral's intentions was fresher, might claim greater weight than Zegers's later readings. Against this count several facts: it's not known what source texts Dana provided to the editors; it's probable, since the published versions vary, that the editors, and perhaps Dana herself, adjusted the copy for style; and unlike Zegers and his colleagues, the editors did not have the benefit of studying Mistral's working papers. Zegers's text is in most cases more inclusive than the earlier versions. He, of course, also made editorial judgments, including, on occasion, silently inserting punctuation and line and stanza breaks.

I began, then, with Zegers's text, noting (as he did) unresolved variants in the typescript. I accepted some but not all of his silent additions (mostly line-end punctuation), noting only those differences that affected sense. In the few instances where my reading of the typescript differed from his (especially where the earlier published sources concur), the text reflects my judgment, and the differences are noted, as are variants from the published sources listed above. The text of the final stanza of Zegers's version of "Electra" and of one stanza of Cáceres's version of "La contadora," both of which I read as canceled in the typescript, have been moved to the notes. The 1942 *La Nación* version of "La trocada" differs sufficiently from the later ones that I have included its entire text in the notes for comparison.

Texts for the other two uncollected poems in what von dem Bussche called, in his prologue to *Reino,* the "powerful 'Mujeres griegas' cycle" largely follow the versions of poet and critic Roque Esteban Scarpa. "Clitemnestra" appeared in the first volume of his *La desterrada en su patría* (Santiago: Editorial Nascimento, 1977). "Casandra" was published the previous year, in *Una mujer nada de tonto* (Santiago: Andrés Bello, 1976). Scarpa offers little detail about his sources. About "Casandra" he says: "From several drafts, this final version of Gabriela's poem has emerged, which we present without supplying verses, but rather ordering them, and still less distorting the free sense that she gave of this clairvoyant and, above all, enamored woman."[6] Scarpa's compilations of these poems have been widely cited. After reviewing the numerous holograph drafts of both poems on microfilm (series I, reels 2 and 15), I see no reason to challenge his "ordering," apart from a single variant reading, which I have noted.

The Santiago daily *El Mercurio* published a different version of "Casandra," without documentation, under the headline "Two Unpublished Poems Found in the Microfilms" on July 22, 2007.

---

6 "De varios borradores, ha salido esta versión final que damos del poema de Gabriela, sin intentar versos, sino ordenándolos, y, menos aún, desvirtuando el sentido libre que ella da de esta mujer vidente, pero sobre todo, enamorada."

NOTES

LA OTRA

Mistral opened the 1954 first edition of *Lagar* with a prologue consisting solely of this poem, separate from the poems gathered under the rubric "Locas mujeres." In preparing her *Poesías completas* (1958), she placed it at the head of the series.

Line 10 *ojo de agua:* literally "eye of water," a spring.

Line 13 *de aliento de su boca:* for a similar formula see, for example, Psalm 33:6 ("By the word of the LORD were the heavens made; and all the host of them by the breath of his mouth" [Authorized Version]).

Line 14 *brasa de su cara:* compare with Isaiah 6:6–7, in which Isaiah's prophetic vocation is sealed: "Then flew one of the seraphims unto me, having a live coal in his hand, *which* he had taken with the tongs from off the altar. / And he laid *it* upon my mouth, and said, Lo, this hath touched thy lips; and thine iniquity is taken away, and thy sin is purged" (Authorized Version).

Line 24 *entraña:* literally "entrail"; a strong word sometimes used metonymically as an endearment (*entrañas mías*), as one might use "my heart."

LA ABANDONADA

Dedication Emma Godoy (1918–89) was a Mexican philosopher, educator, biographer, and award-winning novelist who taught in academic institutions including the Escuela Normal Superior and the Claustro de Sor Juana from 1947 until her retirement in 1973. She collaborated on several cultural journals and became a popular radio broadcaster. An activist on behalf of the aged, she served on many national and international committees. Among her books was a biography of Gabriela Mistral.

Line 2 *acedía:* also the cardinal sin of sloth.

Line 20 *mordidas:* literally "bitten," emaciated, hungry.

Line 24 *granada viva:* also "live grenade."

Line 53 *apurado:* also "exhausted," "consumed," "refined" (as metal).

LA BAILARINA

Line 9 *caer de cuello, de seno y de alma:* 1954 edition has *caer de cuello y de seno y de alma.*

Line 33 *roja veste envenenada:* compare with Nessus's shirt; see Ovid *Metamorphoses* 9:89–210.

LA DESVELADA

Line 8 *sierva:* often "slave," *siervo/a* also signifies one who professes religious orders. *Siervo/a de Dios* (servant of God) is a formula used for any observant Roman Catholic, and specifically one for whom a process of canonization has been started.

Line 23 *medusa:* a jellyfish.

LA DICHOSA

Dedication Paulita Brook (1904–58) was the pseudonym of Mexican playwright, novelist, and critic Lucila Baillet Pallán-León. Married to U.S.-born accountant Arnold Harmony, she formed a close literary and personal relationship with exiled Spanish writer Benjamín Jarnés. Brook was active in the republican exile community in Mexico City, publishing in its journals and serving on the first board of directors for the Ateneo Español de Mexico, an intellectual and cultural institute modeled on the Ateneo de Madrid.

LA FERVOROSA

Line 4 *el faisán que cayó desde los cielos:* this image literalizes the locution *caído del cielo* (heaven-sent), used of unexpected good fortune or opportunity.

Line 28 *mi único Valle:* the valley of Elqui, Mistral's childhood home in the region of Norte Chico.

Line 43 *agoniza:* "bother, harass"; also to attend the dying. In the intransitive form, the act of dying, used also of a fading fire. Mistral recruits all these resonances.

Line 53 *hornaza:* small furnace used by jewelers and other founders to melt and cast metal.

LA FUGITIVA

Line 15 *peana:* in Catholic sanctuary furniture, a step or platform supporting the altar table, or the pedestal supporting a crucifix or saint's image.

Line 37 *ronda:* a children's ring dance; the song or chant to which it is performed; the circle of participants, forming a company.

Line 29 *Las fichas vivas: vivas* can also mean "living" or "live," a sense clearly in play here.

Line 35 *cubre:* 1954 edition has *lame.*

Dedication The physician Eduardo Cruz Coke (1899–1974) was a pioneer of biomedical research and scientific education in Chile. He served as minister of health from 1937 to 1938; his public health programs focused on improved diet and preventive medicine, successfully reducing maternal and infant mortality and chronic illness among working people. He was elected senator for the Conservative Party in 1941 and 1949 and ran as a presidential candidate in 1946.
Martha and Mary were the sisters of Lazarus. The poem's situation derives from Luke 10:38–42: "Now it came to pass, as they went, that he entered into a certain village: and a certain woman named Martha received him into her house. And she had a sister, called Mary, which also sat at Jesus' feet, and heard his word. But Martha was cumbered about much serving, and came to him, and said, Lord, dost thou not care that my sister hath left me to serve alone? bid her therefore that she help me. And Jesus answered and said unto her, Martha, Martha, thou art careful and troubled about many things: But one thing is needful: and Mary hath chosen that good part, which shall not be taken away from her" (Authorized Version).

Line 5 *pino de Alepo:* Aleppo pine (*Pinus halepensis*), Spanish common name *pino de carrasco,* native to the Mediterranean basin and named for the ancient Syrian city of Aleppo.

Dedication Victoria Kent (1898–1987) was Spain's first woman lawyer, representative in Congress, and general director of prisons. At the end of the Spanish Civil War she went to Paris to assist Spanish refugees; when the city fell to the Germans, she was trapped there and spent several years under house arrest. She later lived in Mexico and then the United States, where she worked for the United Nations.
Line 28 *de queja y queja:* follows the 1954 edition; the Aguilar 1968 edition has *se queja y queja.*

Line 61 *Cuando rueda la nieve:* 1954 edition has *Y cuando rueda la nieve.*

Line 65 *él ríe, ríe a mi nombre:* 1954 edition has *el ríe entero a mi nombre.*

Line 68 *contar como David todos sus huesos:* see Psalm 22:16–18: "For dogs have compassed me: / the assembly of the wicked have inclosed me: / they pierced my hands and my feet. / I may tell all my bones: they look *and* stare upon me. / They part my garments among them, / and cast lots upon my vesture" (Authorized Version).

UNA PIADOSA

Line 1 *hombre del faro:* Mistral declines the word *torrero,* "lighthouse keeper."

ANTÍGONA

Lines 1–2 *la fuente Dircea:* The Dircean spring, a spring in Thebes. Named for Lycus's wife Dirce, who was killed by the two sons of Antiope and Zeus (Amphion and Zethus, who later built the walls of the city) for her mistreatment of their mother. They tied Dirce's hair to the horns of a bull and then threw her battered body into the spring that afterward bore her name.

Line 18 *caña cascada que lo afirma:* It was Oedipus who had solved the riddle of the Sphinx (What goes on four legs in the morning, two at noon, and three in the evening?) and here enacts the answer.

Line 22 *donde ya no puedas:* idiomatically, "where you can't anymore" or "where you can go no further." The line can also be construed "where now you may not." The site of the poem's action is not specified, but at Colonus the old king sends his daughter away from the place where he will die, telling her that it is forbidden for her to see what will happen or for him to tell anyone but Theseus the precise location. This context may inform the second sense of the line (see Sophocles, *Oedipus at Colonus,* scene 8).

LA CABELLUDA

In the corrected typescript of *Lagar II,* this poem opens with the lines

Vimos nacer, vimos crecer
y vimos madurar violenta

of which the first has been struck through. Beside them appears the typed alternative opening

yo vi nacer, yo vi crecer
y madurar, y vi de muerta

a la tocada, a la tapada
y vestida de cabellera.

Line 14 *Rostro ni voz: voz* is typed above the presumably earlier *porte,*
which is uncanceled.

Line 18 *En el abrazo nos miraba:* typed alternative is *Nos inundaba con su
abrazo.*

Line 53 *mano terca y llama en greñas:* typed alternative is *la greña en llamas,
la mano terca;.*

Line 72 *En una caja de cristales:* typed alternative is *En una caja de vidrio duro.*

LA CONTADORA

Line 11 *Zumban, hierven y abejean:* Cáceres includes the previous typescript
line, which Zegers reads as canceled: *Tantas son que no dan respiro, /
zumban, hierven y abejean.*

Line 13 *y contadas tampoco me dejan:* Cáceres has *y contadas tampoco dejan . . .*

Line 18 *Pero el mar que cuenta siempre:* before this line Cáceres inserts a
stanza break, not in the typescript or Zegers.

Line 19 *y más rendida, más me deja . . . :* Zegers reads the line *más rendida,
nos deja.*

Line 31 *corro:* a ring or singing game like ring-around-a-rosy, thus "cho-
rus." Note similarity with *ronda* elsewhere in the series.

Line 32 *y me atrapan en la rueda:* Cáceres has *y me atrapa en la rueda.* After
this line she inserts the following stanza, canceled in the typescript and
omitted in Zegers:

Los ribereños me cuentan
la ahogada sumida en hierbas
y su mirada cuenta su historia,
y yo las tronco en mis palmas abiertas. [typescript has *y yo
las tomo. . . .*]

Line 33 *Al pulgar llegan las de animales:* in the typescript, *llegan* is written in
what appears to be Mistral's hand above the typed *van viniendo.* Zegers
has *van llegando.*

Line 37 *Los marineros alocados:* Cáceres omits this and the following three
stanzas.

Line 58 *mis brazos una noche entera:* Zegers inserts a stanza break after this
line.

Line 60 *se las voy dando por que recuerde:* Mistral carefully avoids specify-
ing the gender of "the one that I had." I have altered the construction
slightly to avoid an awkward or prejudicial English pronoun choice.

Line 65 *Busco alguna que la recuerde:* Cáceres inserts a stanza break before this line.

Line 3 *que en horas fui mudada: Mundo Nuevo* has *fue mudado.* My text follows the typescript, *La Palabra y el Hombre,* and Zegers.

Line 11 *Ya está más muda que piedra rodada: muda* is typed above the presumably earlier *quieta* in the typescript.

Line 16 *marchando o dormida:* Zegers breaks the line before this phrase or *hemistiquio,* interpreting an ambiguous mark on the typescript line; my text follows *La Palabra* and *Mundo Nuevo* in not breaking the *alejandrino.*

Line 24 *Y cuando Orestes sestee a mi costado: costado* is typed above the presumably earlier *lado.*

Line 27 *las manos de ella que lo enmallataron:* typescript, *La Palabra, Mundo Nuevo,* and Zegers have *enmallotaron,* a spelling not in the dictionary of the Real Academia Española.

Line 38 *A mí y a Orestes:* Zegers has *Y a mí;* my text follows the typescript, *La Palabra,* etc.

Line 38 *nos dejó sin besos: La Palabra* has *no dejó;* my text follows the typescript, Zegers, etc.

Line 54 *El habla niña nos vuelve y resbala:* Zegers inserts a comma after *habla,* not present in the typescript, *La Palabra,* or *Mundo Nuevo.*

Line 57 *Husmea mi camino y ven Orestes:* Zegers omits the stanza break before this line and adds a comma after *ven;* my text follows the typescript, *La Palabra, Mundo Nuevo,* etc.

Line 63 *¿Por qué no duerme al lado del Egisto.:* typed alternative is *Por qué no due[r]me su noche con Egisto. La Palabra* and *Mundo Nuevo* end this line with a closing question mark and open the following line with an inverted question mark; my text follows the typescript and Zegers.

Line 73 *Yo no quiero saber: La Palabra* and *Mundo Nuevo* have *Ya no quiero;* my text follows Zegers's reading of an ambiguous mark near the typed "o" in the typescript.

Line 75 *cómo cayó, qué dijo dando el grito:* Zegers has *del grito;* typescript, *La Palabra,* and *Mundo nueovo* have *el grito.*

Line 76 *y si te dio maldición o te bendijo.:* Zegers inserts a stanza break after this line.

Line 84 *El dios que te movió:* Zegers capitalizes *Dios;* typescript, *La Palabra,* and *Mundo Nuevo* have *dios.*

Line 88 *La niebla tiene pliegues de sudario: La Palabra* has a stanza break before this line; my text follows the typescript, *Mundo Nuevo,* and Zegers.

Line 96 *y vas a mi costado sin palabras,:* Zegers reads *palabra* as singular, the terminal *s* being either faint or partially erased, and follows the typescript in ending the line with a question mark. He inserts a stanza break after this line and employs an initial capital on the next, neither of which is present in the typescript. I interpret the question as continuing, as in *Mundo Nuevo,* and place the closing question mark after *Oreste-Electra,* a line which ends without punctuation in the typescript but with a period in *La Palabra* and *Mundo Nuevo.*

Line 100 *Electra-Oreste, yo, tú, Oreste-Electra:* *La Palabra* and *Mundo Nuevo* have *Electra-Orestes, yo, tú, Orestes-Electra;* this spelling would affect metrical elision, so I have followed the typescript and Zegers.

Line 103 *Pare yo por que puedas detenerte:* Zegers has *porque puedas;* my text follows the typescript, *La Palabra,* and *Mundo Nuevo.*

Line 104 *o yo me tumbe, para detenerte:* *Mundo Nuevo* has *para detener;* my text follows the typescript, *La Palabra,* and Zegers.

Line 114 *y ahora es niebla-albatrós, niebla-camino,:* Zegers condenses this and the following typescript lines to a single composite line: *y ahora es niebla-albatros, niebla-barco.* My text follows the typescript, *La Palabra,* and *Mundo Nuevo.*

In the typescript the poem concludes with the following stanza, which has a light vertical stroke through it. Zegers does not read this as an authoritative cancellation and includes the stanza. My text follows *La Palabra* and *Mundo Nuevo* in omitting it.

> O yo nunca nací, solo
> he soñado padre, madre, y un héroe,
> una casa, la fuente Dircea y Ágora.
> No es cuerpo el que llegó,
> ni potencias.

MADRE BISOJA

Line 9 *Arqueaba el cielo su brazo:* This stanza parallels the Olympian creation myth as given in Hesiod's *Theogony* (126–38) and Apollodorus's *Library and Epitome* (1.1–2); the union of earth and sky via fertile rain also appears in Lucretius (1.250–54) and in Virgil's *Georgics* (2.325–38). Robert Graves in *The Greek Myths* narrates the story as follows: "At the beginning of all things, Mother Earth [Gaea] emerged from Chaos and bore her sun Uranus as she slept. Gazing down fondly at her from the mountains, he showered fertile rain upon her secret clefts, and she bore grass, flowers, and trees, with the beasts and birds proper to each" (rev. ed., London: Penguin, 1960, 1:31).

Line 14 *la Verdeante que la Parda:* Zegers has *la parda,* omitting the type-
script's capital.

Line 61 *Y cuando se le reían: le preguntaban* is typed above *se le reían* and not
canceled.

LA QUE AGUARDA

This poem shares lines and passages with *La ansiosa* as published in *Lagar.*
Several manuscript comments in various hands allude to this fact on the
typescript. Zegers identifies the notes "Dice Gabriela que verá de salvar
alguna estrofa" and "Repetido en 'La ansiosa' " as by Doris Dana. Notes in
other hands include "Partes igual a 'La Ansiosa,' " "Está antes con el titulo
La ansiosa," and "continuación del borrador 12."

Line 38 *y el grito mío no se relaja::* Zegers omits the colon, added manually
in the typsecript.

DOS TRASCORDADOS

Title *trascordado* can mean not only "forgotten" or "irretrievably lost" but
also "to be mistaken by confusing one thing with another."

Line 6 *y husmeados de la loba y la [. . .]:* husmeados is an alternative typed
above *mordidos.* The line is unfinished in the typescript, ending with
three manuscript dashes.

Line 11 *ciegos dormidos y ciegos despiertos:* An annotation in the left margin
beside this stanza, attributed by Zegers to Doris Dana, reads "Dice
Gabriela añadir."

Line 23 *sus pobres manos de su ronda muerta:* typed alternative endings for
this line appear beside it in the right margin: *(de su santa ronda)* and *(de
su vieja ronda).* In this use of *ronda,* Mistral implicates other participants
in the ring dance, thus "dance of death."

In the left margin beside the final stanza, in what appears to be
Mistral's hand, is written the word *Falta.* In the right margin appears
an annotation, attributed by Zegers to Doris Dana: "Dice Gabriela
completar."

LA TROCADA

Line 29 *aprendiendo tierra mudada: aprendiendo* is written in the type-
script above the typed line *y he de aprender tierra mudada,* which is
uncanceled.

Canceled versions of stanzas three and five from the *La Nación* text appear
in the typescript. In the left margin beside the canceled stanza 3, an an-
notation in what appears to be Mistral's hand reads "buscar este verso."
The complete 1942 version printed in *La Nación* follows:

LA TROCADA

Así no fue como me amaban
y ando por eso desatentada.
Serían aquéllos los metales
donde el amor tuvo peana;
serían los tristes líquenes,
el descampado, la venteada.
Acaso eran los sustentos:
(piñon, y cardo y avellana),
que me querían como se odia
y al mismo Amor avergonzaban.

El montañés tuvo mi rostro
por una ruta con celada.
Fuí para él loba y raposa,
por matorrales rastreada.
Veía el duende de la niebla,
los cristales de la avalancha,
y no miró mi ceibo ardiendo
sobre su puerta con escarcha.

Se me levantan como juncos
pisoteados las espaldas.
Bato cabellos alborotados
por este viento de la infancia.
Creen mi llanto, creen mi risa;
me llaman gozo y confianza,
y ya no grito cuando duermo,
de ser en sueños renegada.

En el país de la gaviota,
del aire suyo voy llevada,
y preguntase al que me lleva
por qué bajando fué trocada,
por qué me creen en las dunas,
por qué en arena y sal me aman.

Pero mi voz la tengo nueva
como alondra recién cazada,
y esta mi voz amanecida
horas y días calla y calla,

de no saber si es el amor
o de qué nombre se le llama.

Pues lo que fué así no era
y hay que aprender tierra mudada,
clara patria color de leche,
lento olivar, lindas aguadas.
Y hay que ensayar toda la vida
como unas ropas trastrocadas,
con extrañeza, con asombro
y azoro de resucitada.

CLITEMNESTRA

Line 52 *No te vea yo más:* Scarpa has *No te vea ya más.* In the manuscript
  drafts of the poem from Mistral's notebooks I read *yo,* which preserves
  parallelism (see series I, reel 2, book 1, p. 33).

Line 66 *cobrando:* also "collecting," as a debt, or a sacrifice owed.

CASANDRA

Line 97 *Ya estamos ya las dos:* Cassandra and her homeland.

SELECTED BIBLIOGRAPHY

POETRY

Desolación: Poemas. New York: Instituto de las Españas, 1922.

Lagar. Santiago: Editorial del Pacífico, 1954.

Lagar II. Edited by Pedro Pablo Zegers and Ana María Cuneo. Santiago: Dirección de Bibliotecas, Archivos y Museos, Biblioteca Nacional, 1991.

Locas mujeres. Santiago: LOM Ediciones, 2003.

Poema de Chile. Barcelona: Pomaire, 1967.

Poesías completas. Edited by Margaret Bates; introduction by Esther de Cáceres. Madrid: Aguilar, 1958; 4th ed. rev. 1968.

Tala. Buenos Aires: SUR, 1938; reprint Santiago: Andrés Bello, 1979.

Ternura. Madrid: Saturnino Calleja, 1924; rev. Buenos Aires: Espasa-Calpe, 1945.

ENGLISH TRANSLATIONS AND BILINGUAL EDITIONS

Burns, Paul, and Salvador Ortiz-Carboneres, trans. *Gabriela Mistral: Selected Poems.* Oxford: Oxbow Books, 2006.

Dana, Doris, trans. *Selected Poems of Gabriela Mistral.* Baltimore: Johns Hopkins University Press, 1971.

Giachetti, Maria, trans. *A Gabriela Mistral Reader.* Edited by Marjorie Agosín. Fredonia, NY: White Pine, 1993.

Hughes, Langston, trans. *Selected Poems of Gabriela Mistral.* Bloomington: Indiana University Press, 1957.

Kyle, Christiane Jacox, trans. *Poemas de las madres / The Mothers' Poems, by Gabriela Mistral.* Cheney: Eastern Washington University Press, 1995.

Le Guin, Ursula K., trans. *Selected Poems of Gabriela Mistral.* Albuquerque: University of New Mexico Press, 2003.

Tapscott, Stephen, ed. and trans. *Gabriela Mistral: Selected Prose and Prose-Poems.* Austin: University of Texas Press, 2002.

PUBLISHED CORRESPONDENCE

Cartas. Vol. 3 of *Antología mayor, Gabriela Mistral.* Edited by Luis Vargas Saavedra. Santiago: Lord Cochrane, 1992.

This America of Ours: The Letters of Gabriela Mistral and Victoria Ocampo. Edited and translated by Elizabeth Horan and Doris Meyer. Austin: University of Texas Press, 2003.

Vuestra Gabriela: Cartas inéditas de Gabriela Mistral a los Errázuriz Echenique y Tomic Errázuriz. Edited with preface and notes by Luis Vargas Saavedra. Santiago: Zig-Zag, 1995.

BIOGRAPHICAL STUDIES

Arce de Vázquez, Margot. *Gabriela Mistral: The Poet and Her Work.* Translated by Helene Masslo Anderson. New York: New York University Press, 1964.

Figueroa, Virgilio. *La divina Gabriela.* Santiago: Impreso El Esfuerzo, 1933.

Fiol-Matta, Licia. *A Queer Mother for the Nation: The State and Gabriela Mistral.* Minneapolis: University of Minnesota Press, 2002.

Gazarian-Gautier, Marie-Lise. "Gabriela Mistral: La maestra de Elqui." In *Vida y obra,* vol. 4 of *Antología mayor, Gabriela Mistral.* Santiago: Lord Cochrane, 1992.

Horan, Elizabeth. *Gabriela Mistral: An Artist and Her People.* Washington, DC: Organization of American States, 1994.

BIBLIOGRAPHY AND CRITICAL COLLECTIONS

Agosín, Marjorie, ed. *Gabriela Mistral: The Audacious Traveler.* Athens: Ohio University Press, 2003.

Lillo, Gastón, and J. Guillermo Renart, with Naín Nómez, eds. *Re-leer hoy a Gabriela Mistral: Mujer, historia, y sociedad en América Latina.* Ottawa: University of Ottawa and Editorial Universidad de Santiago, 1997.

Olea, Raquel, and Soledad Fariña, eds. *Una palabra cómplice: Encuentro con Gabriela Mistral.* Santiago: Corporación de Desarrollo de la Mujer La Morada, Editorial Cuarto Propio, Isis Internacional, 1997.

Rubio, Patricia. *Gabriela Mistral ante la crítica: Bibliografía anotada.* Santiago: Universitaria / Dirección de Bibliotecas, Archivos y Museos, 1995.

INDEX OF FIRST LINES